RAILWAYS OF BRITAIN

Devon and Cornwall

Colin and David McCarthy

Ian Allan
PUBLISHING

CONTENTS

First published 2008

ISBN 978 0 7110 3302 3

Front cover: 'Battle of Britain' No 34066 *Spitfire* heads an up service from Ilfracombe over the River Taw towards Barnstaple Junction station.
R. C. Riley

Previous page: One of the most significant engineering works undertaken for the construction of the Cornwall Railway was the Royal Albert Bridge crossing the Tamar at Saltash. Here the up 'Riviera Express' is recorded heading over the bridge.
Ian Allan Library

© Colin McCarthy, David McCarthy and Michael Cobb 2008
Series Editor: Peter Waller

Published by Ian Allan Publishing

an imprint of Ian Allan Publishing Ltd, Hersham, Surrey KT12 4RG.

Printed by Ian Allan Printing Ltd, Hersham, Surrey KT12 4RG.

Code: 0807/C

Visit the Ian Allan Publishing website at: www.ianallanpublishing.com

INTRODUCTION

In 2003, Colonel Michael Cobb published his superb two-volume atlas covering the railways of Great Britain. This work, widely praised when first published and subsequently reprinted and then reissued as a revised second edition, forms the basis of the cartography in this, the third of new series that is designed to provide a comprehensive historical guide to the railways of the country.

The cartography shows the railway infrastructure of the counties concerned, differentiating the lines built between those open for passenger services, those open for freight only, those preserved and those closed completely. Alongside the railways, the major roads of the area are also shown so that readers can identify the inter-relationship between road and rail transport.

When compiling his original books, Michael Cobb decided to exclude those lines that were not constructed by the main line companies; these tended to be predominantly industrial lines; the intention here is to incorporate as many of these lines as possible. Unlike other areas, Devon and Cornwall, being predominantly agrarian, lacked the large numbers of industrial railways that were a feature of areas such as the Lancashire coalfield; there were, however, a number, such as the Lee Moor Tramway, and these are covered within the book's pages. Also included in an indication of locomotive sheds, fuller details of each of the sheds featured can be found in the book's narrative.

Supplementing the cartography, the book also includes an outline history of the lines featured accompanied by a representative selection of photographs portraying the railway locations discussed. The book concludes with a full gazetteer of all the stations featured, giving opening and closing dates, as well as information about renaming if appropriate.

Notes on the maps

The maps are based upon the original work undertaken by Colonel Michael Cobb for his atlas; individual symbols are described within the key. The railway routes shown are differentiated between the lines that are open to passenger services, those that are open to freight traffic only, preserved lines and those closed completely. Station names with earlier versions are given; fuller details of the opening and closing dates of the stations can be found in the index and gazetteer included at the back of the book. The major road network is shown as a means of placing the open and closed lines into their local context; the book, however, is not a road atlas and therefore minor roads are excluded.

OVERVIEW

Although railway development in the counties of Devon and Cornwall ultimately became dominated by the machinations of the Great Western and London & South Western railways, the history of railways in the region stretches back to the dawn of the industrial age.

The industrial – and railway – history of the area is dominated by geology and geography. The geology, rich in exploitable minerals like stone, tin and china clay, was the spur to the development of many of the early mineral railways, particularly in Cornwall, whilst geography, with the rugged coastline, fishing harbours and holiday resorts as well as the large expanses of Dartmoor and Exmoor, was to determine where many of the future main lines were to be constructed.

The earliest railways to be promoted were largely designed to transport minerals from mine or quarry to port; it was the promotion of the Bodmin & Wenford Railway – the first line in Cornwall to use locomotive power – in the 1830s that started the evolution of a network of lines to serve the counties. Initially, courtesy of the Bristol & Exeter, South Devon – the latter with its experimental use of atmospheric power – and Cornwall Railways, it was the broad gauge that came to dominate the region. But gauge and railway politics ensured that, once the London & South Western Railway became interested in the development of railways in North Devon, that the standard gauge made its appearance. The histories of the individual railway companies that came to play a role in the development of the local railway network are narrated in the next section; suffice here to note that the GWR ultimately came to dominate South Devon and Cornwall whilst the LSWR operated the majority of lines to North Devon and to the coast of North Cornwall. The somewhat isolated LSWR lines became commonly known as the 'Withered Arm'; physically separated from the rest of the LSWR network, the company relied upon Working Powers on the section of the GWR between Exeter St David's and Cowley Bridge Junction in order to gain access to them.

At the height of the railway age there was considerable competition between these two great railway companies. From Barnstaple, for example, both operated services towards London: the GWR from Victoria Road station via Taunton and the LSWR via Exeter to Waterloo. From Plymouth, both competed on the ocean liner traffic from stations in the harbour until agreement saw the traffic concentrated with the GWR.

By the late 19th century, many of the mineral resources from which the region derived much of its wealth were already in terminal decline, with many of the exclusively freight-only mineral lines disappearing, but by this date new traffic in the form of holidaymakers to the coast was beginning to be a major influence on the railway industry. Whilst, however, this traffic could significantly increase revenue during the summer months, during the winter passenger traffic over many of the lines was sparse.

At the Grouping in 1923, the LSWR passed to the Southern Railway whilst the GWR – expanded through acquisition – remained, thus ensuring a further generation of competition to and from the West Country. It was no coincidence that two of the companies' most prestigious trains – the SR's 'Atlantic Coast Express' and the GWR's 'Cornish Riviera Express' – both operated to and from destinations in Devon and Cornwall.

In 1948, with the Nationalisation of the railways, everything initially remained as before, with the Southern and Western regions inheriting the assets of the SR and GWR respectively but with Nationalisation came the opportunity for rationalisation. Indicative of this was the concentration of all services in Launceston at the old LSWR station and the closure of the ex-GWR one. As the economics of the railway industry continued to deteriorate, the southwest of England was not immune. Passenger services were cut from a number of branches and efforts made, through the introduction of new diesel units allied to new halts, to bolster the finances of those lines that did survive. The transfer of the erstwhile LSWR lines to WR control in 1963 meant that for the first time all lines in Devon and Cornwall were now under single management. This allowed for further rationalisation.

By the early 1960s, and the Beeching Report, much of the passenger network in Devon and Cornwall was under threat; many lines, in particular those of the 'Withered Arm', were to succumb although a small number of routes did manage to avoid closure. Today, the southwest has a substantial passenger network. Apart from the ex-GWR main line from Penzance to Exeter and Taunton, there remain passenger branches to St Ives, Falmouth, Newquay, Looe, Gunnislake, Paignton, Barnstaple and Exmouth as well as the ex-LSWR main line from Exeter to Salisbury. Today the majority of services are handled by the First Great Western franchise although both South West Trains and CrossCountry also operate into the region. There are also a number of thriving preservation schemes, featuring both standard and narrow gauge operation.

Two hundred years ago, at the start of the railway revolution, it was the mineral traffic that provided the spur to the development of a major network of lines in Devon and Cornwall. As these abstractive industries have declined, many of the lines associated with them have closed as well. There remains, however, a significant amount of freight traffic – such as china clay – carried over the railways in the area although in the 21st century this is but a shadow of former levels.

Left: Following the withdrawal of passenger services from Coleford Junction to Plymouth, and the north Cornwall lines, via Okehampton, the former Southern route was kept open for the shipment of stone from the quarry at Meldon. On 1 March 1983, Class 47 No 47479 heads west through the long-closed station at North Tawton with a service of empties from Exeter Riverside to Meldon. *Peter Medley*

HISTORY

Axminster & Lyme Regis Light Railway

There had been proposals for the construction of a line to Lyme Regis for many years, but it was not until 15 June 1899 that a Light Railway Order for the A&LRLR was obtained. Services over the 6.75-mile long branch commenced on 24 August 1903. In 1910 there were eight return workings each weekday with no Sunday service. A single trip, calling at the one intermediate station at Combpyne, took 20min. In 1930, the crossing loop at Combpyne was removed. For many years, until withdrawal in 1961, the branch was home to the last three surviving examples of the Adams-designed 'Radial' tanks. Freight over the branch was withdrawn on 3 February 1964 and the line closed completely with the withdrawal of passenger services on 29 November 1965.

Right: In May 1952, one of the Adams-designed 'Radial' tanks for which the Lyme Regis branch was noted — No 30584 — is pictured at Axminster station.
Ian Allan Library

Right: The 11.35am service from Axminster to Lyme Regis pictured crossing Cannington Viaduct behind No 30582 on 29 August 1953.
S. C. Nash

Barnstaple & Ilfracombe Railway

Incorporated on 4 July 1870, the B&IR was a subsidiary of the LSWR and opened on 20 July 1874. The line, just over 14 miles in length, was steeply graded, with sections at 1 in 40 and 1 in 36, and was operated from the start by the LSWR. The line from Barnstaple to Ilfracombe, but not the bridge across the River Taw, was doubled between 1889 and 1891. In 1910 there were 10 return workings per weekday with two on Sundays. The single journey time was just under 40min. Freight services over the line ceased on 7 September 1964 and, in December 1967, the line was singled. Although a holiday destination, Ilfracombe was ill-served by the railways and was an easy target for the growing road transport industry. Passenger services over the line were

Left: In July 1964, Ivatt 2-6-2T No 41290 stands in Ilfracombe station awaiting departure with a service to Barnstaple. *Ian Allan Library*

Left: On 18 May 1959 'Battle of Britain' class No 34072 *257 Squadron* is recorded marshalling stock at Ilfracombe station. *K. L. Cook*

withdrawn on 5 October 1970 although there were initial efforts to reopen the
line as a preservation scheme. These, however, failed and the line was
subsequently lifted.

Bere Alston & Calstock Railway

Originally promoted as a 3ft 6in gauge light railway, the BA&CR – a subsidiary
of the Plymouth, Devonport & South Western Junction Railway – was

Left: In October 1963, about two years before the line closed to passenger services, Ivatt 2-6-2T No 41224 is pictured departing from Barnstaple Junction station with the 3.15pm service to Torrington. *R. Mee*

authorised under a Light Railway Order of 12 July 1905 to provide a link between Bere Alston and the East Cornwall Mineral Railway at Calstock. A further order, dated 12 October 1905, authorised the construction of the line as standard gauge and the branch opened on 2 March 1908. Freight over the line ceased in February 1966 but the section from Bere Alston to Calstock remains open for passenger services with the current franchisee, First Great Western, operating the branch between Plymouth and Gunnislake.

Bideford Extension Railway

A 6.5-mile long extension of the North Devon Railway & Dock Co from Fremington to Bideford, the BER was authorised on 4 August 1853. The line, leased by Thomas Brassey, was opened on 2 November 1855. The LSWR took over the lease on 1 August 1862 and, following an Act of 25 July 1864, took over the company on 1 January 1865. The line, originally built as broad gauge, was converted to mixed gauge by 1 March 1863 when the first standard gauge train from Barnstaple to Bideford operated. The line was extended to Torrington on 18 July 1872. Powers to remove the broad gauge lines were obtained on 13 July 1876. In 1910 there were 10 return workings each weekday with two on Sundays between Barnstaple and Torrington; the journey time for the single 14.25-mile long journey was about 30min. Passenger services over the route were withdrawn on 4 October 1965 although freight traffic over the section from Barnstaple to Torrington was to survive until 5 March 1983. The route is now converted into a cycleway.

Bideford, Westward Ho! & Appledore Railway

Incorporated on 21 May 1896, the standard gauge – but isolated – BWH&AR was opened in two stages: from Bideford to Northam on 24 April 1901 and from Northam to Appledore on 1 May 1908. The later section was constructed under a Light Railway Order, which allowed the railway to dispense with level crossing gates on this section. There were 10 return workings per weekday in 1910,

Right: With the quay in the middle distance, Ivatt 2-6-2T No 41210 is recorded heading into Fremington station with a service from Torrington to Waterloo. The section of line beyond Barnstaple Junction to Torrington, via Fremington, was the last part of the route to Halwill Junction to remain operational, with freight traffic surviving until 1983.
J. C. Beckett

Right: North British-built diesel-hydraulic No D6339 passes a fine example of an ex-LSWR lower-quadrant starting signal as it runs into Torrington station on the freight-only branch from Barnstaple with a brake van to collect some milk tank wagons on 22 July 1970. A further rationalisation of the route was later to see the signalling at Torrington removed.
G. F. Gilham

with 11 on Tuesdays and Saturdays but none on Sundays. A single journey over the seven-mile line took 30min. Although traffic was occasionally heavy, disputes with Bideford Town Council and the overall poor finances of the company led to the line's closure on 28 March 1917. The line's locomotives and other equipment were requisitioned by the government for the war effort.

Bodmin & Wadebridge Railway

The first railway in Cornwall to be operated by locomotive, the Bodmin & Wenford was incorporated on 23 May 1832. The line, designed to carry ore to the harbour at Wadebridge, was opened from Wadebridge to Dunmere on 4 July 1834. The branch to Bodmin opened on the same day. The section from Dunmere to Wenford Bridge opened on 30 September 1834 as did the branch to Ruthern Bridge. The LSWR illegally acquired the line in 1846 — a position

Below: Boscarne Junction was the point at which the Bodmin & Wenford line met the GWR line from Bodmin Road via Bodmin General. On 22 September 1959 one of the three surviving Beattie well-tanks, No 30585, runs back past the LSWR signalbox at the junction during the shunting of the Wadebridge train. *P. Q. Treloar*

11

that was not regularised until an Act of 25 June 1886 — and was operated as an isolated outpost of the railway until the opening of the North Cornwall line to Wadebridge on 1 November 1895. In 1910 there were 10 workings between Bodmin and Wadebridge on weekdays with 11 in the reverse direction; there was no Sunday service. Services were allowed just under 20min for the 6.5-mile long journey. The line from Dunmere to Wenford Bridge and the Ruthern Bridge branch were to carry freight traffic only through their career; the latter was to close officially on 30 December 1933 following the operation of the last train on 29 November the same year. Passenger services over the North Cornwall line ceased in 1966 and the remaining passenger services over the line — from Bodmin North to Padstow and from Bodmin Road to Boscarne Junction — ceased on 30 January 1967. At this date, the sections of line from Wadebridge to Padstow and from Dunmere to Bodmin North closed completely. The section of line from Wadebridge to Wadebridge Quay closed on 2 April 1973. The section from Boscarne Junction to Wadebridge closed completely on 4 September 1978. The last clay traffic from Wenford Bridge departed in September 1983 and the line from there to Boscarne Junction was officially closed on 18 November 1983.

Bristol & Exeter Railway

Authorised as a broad gauge line on 19 May 1836, the Bristol & Exeter was engineered by Isambard Kingdom Brunel. However, the company soon found itself in financial difficulties and was leased to the GWR in order to enable operations to commence. Having opened as far as Taunton on 1 July 1842, the line was extended to Exeter on 1 May 1844. Following the expiry of the GWR's lease in 1849, the B&ER commenced its own operations and expanded thereafter by absorbing a number of smaller concerns, such as the Exe Valley Railway in 1875. A third line — to enable the operation of standard gauge trains — was added in the mid-1870s; standard gauge freight trains from Taunton to Exeter commenced operation in March 1876 with passenger services commencing the following year. On 1 January 1876 the GWR again assumed operation of the line, absorbing the smaller company as a result of an Act of 27 June 1876. The line from Exeter to Bristol remains operational as part of the ex-GWR main line with passenger services predominantly provided by the First Great Western franchise. Apart from the main line, the B&ER also constructed a number of branches. These included:

- Tiverton Junction-Tiverton — The 4.75-mile long branch from Tiverton Junction to Tiverton opened as a broad gauge route on 12 June 1848. The branch was converted to standard gauge in 1884 prior to the opening of the Tiverton & North Devon Railway. In 1910 there were 12 journeys from Tiverton to the junction and 13 back on weekdays with an additional service on Tuesdays. There were two return workings on Sundays. The journey time for a single trip was around 10min. Passenger services over the line ceased on 5 October 1964 and the line was to close completely on 5 June 1967.

Above: Viewed looking in the down direction, this view shows Tiverton Junction in 1921. Opened originally on 1 May 1844, the station was known as Tiverton Road until the opening of the Tiverton branch on 12 June 1848. The branch to Hemyock was opened on 29 May 1876 and coaches for the latter service can be seen under the footbridge on the left. The station was to be rebuilt a decade later when the lines through it were quadrupled.
Ian Allan Library

Buckfastleigh, Totnes & South Devon Railway

Initially incorporated on 25 June 1864 to construct a line from Totnes to Buckfastleigh, powers were obtained the following year to extend to Ashburton. The broad gauge branch, almost 10 miles in length, along with the associated line to the quay at Totnes, opened on 1 May 1872 and was worked by the South Devon Railway; it was converted to standard gauge in May 1892. The line was acquired by the GWR on 1 July 1892. Passenger services over the route were withdrawn on 3 November 1958 and freight on 10 September 1962. The branch was preserved by the Dart Valley Railway and initially services ran through to Ashburton; however, road improvements meant that the section between Buckfastleigh and Ashburton was again to close, this time permanently, on 2 October 1971.

Budleigh Salterton Railway

Authorised on 20 July 1894, the 6.5-mile long line from Tipton St Johns to Budleigh Salterton was opened on 15 May 1897. Operated by the LSWR, the larger company promoted an extension to Exmouth, which opened on 1 June 1903. The LSWR absorbed the BSR following an Act of 18 August 1911. Passenger services over the line were withdrawn on 6 March 1967 on which date the route was to close completely.

Callington & Calstock Railway

The C&CR was authorised on 9 August 1869 to construct a line, using the trackbed of the earlier Tamar, Kit Hill & Callington Railway, for eight miles

Above: On 2 July 1957, 16 months before the withdrawal of passenger services over the branch from Totnes, Collett-designed 0-4-2T No 1427 awaits departure from Ashburton station.

R. C. Riley/Transport Treasury

between the two settlements. Before the 3ft 6in gauge line was opened, however, it changed its name on 25 May 1871 to the East Cornwall Mineral Railway.

Cornwall Central Railway

This was originally incorporated in 1864 as the Launceston, Bodmin & Wadebridge Railway but changed its name on 6 July 1865 to the CCR following authorisation of an extension to Ruthern Bridge. However, the line was never to be built and much of the route was subsequently covered by the North Cornwall Railway.

Cornwall Railway

Authorised on 3 August 1846 with backing from the Bristol & Exeter, Great Western and South Devon railways, the broad gauge Cornwall Railway opened from Truro to Plymouth, where it joined up with the South Devon Railway at Millbay station, on 2 May 1859 officially, and to the public two days later. Amongst the significant engineering work undertaken in connection with the line was the Royal Albert Bridge at Saltash, which provided a direct link across the Tamar between Devon and Cornwall. The branch to Falmouth opened to passengers on 24 August 1863 and to freight on the following 5 October. From Truro towards Penwithers Junction the single-track broad gauge line ran parallel to the existing standard gauge line of the West Cornwall Railway; at Penwithers Junction, the CR line cut across the West Cornwall Railway's line

Left: On 27 November 1974 'Western' class diesel-hydraulic No 1035 *Western Yeoman* is recorded departing from Truro station with the 09.30 service from Paddington to Penzance. By this date the locomotive was approaching the end of its career; it was withdrawn in January 1975 and scrapped some 18 months later. *Brian Morrison*

to Newham. The Cornwall Railway's independent existence ceased with an Act of 24 June 1889 after which it was absorbed into the GWR, a company that had operated the line since 1 January 1877. Following conversion to standard gauge, the line from Plymouth — with the exception of the west to south curve at Plymouth that gave access to Millbay station, which closed completely on

Left: On 20 May 1975 Class 47 No 47266 passes through Bodmin Road with a fully-fitted freight destined for Scottish Region. The branch to Bodmin itself, then still in regular use, can be seen heading to the north adjacent to the up platform in the station. *Peter J. Robinson*

13 January 1964 — to Truro remains as part of the ex-GWR main line to Penzance, whilst the branch to Falmouth is also still open for passenger services, although for a brief period in the early 1970s, the branch was cut back to a terminus — now known as Falmouth Town (and previously as The Dell) — some half a mile short of the original terminus. When services were extended back to the original station in 1975, the terminus was renamed Falmouth Docks. Passenger services are today handled by the First Great Western franchise. Falmouth Docks were connected to the branch in 1861.

Cornwall Minerals Railway

Formed by a speculator, W. R. Roebuck, interested in exploiting the boom in the china clay industry, the Cornwall Minerals Railway was authorised by an Act of 21 July 1873 to take-over or construct a total of some 46.75 miles of line, all of which were opened on 1 June 1874. The routes concerned were as follows:

- Fowey-Newquay — this incorporated sections of two earlier lines — Par-Bugle and Newquay-St Dennis (Hendra Crazy) — although the original incline at Carmears was bypassed with a new heavily graded section of line from Pontsmill to Luxulyan. A short section of the original line at Pontsmill was retained to serve Pontsmill Clay Works. In April 1910 the line was operated in two sections: from Par to Newquay, with five return workings per weekday and no Sunday service; and, Par-Fowey, with a reversal at St Blazey, seeing five return workings per weekday with again no Sunday service. For Newquay-Par the journey time for a single 20.75-mile trip was just under an hour at best; from Par to Fowey, the

Left: In August 1953, '45xx' class No 4570 awaits departure from Falmouth with a service to Truro.
Ian Allan Library

Left: The somewhat basic facilities provided at the interim terminus of the Falmouth branch are evident in this view of the station, by now renamed Falmouth Town, taken on 5 June 1988, which shows the 16.00 service from Truro to Falmouth Dock approaching the platform.
Nigel Hunt

4.5-mile long trip took just under 20min. Passenger services on the line from St Blazey to Fowey were withdrawn on 8 July 1929, although workmen's services continued until 31 December 1934. Following agreement with English China Clays, the line from St Blazey to Fowey was to close completely on 1 July 1968 with the exception of the short section from St Blazey to Par Harbour that remains operational. The Par-Newquay line remains open, with passenger services provided primarily by First Great Western.

- Bugle-Carbis Wharf – This short line from Goonbarrow Junction was to close officially from 31 December 1989. There remains an English China Clay works at Goonbarrow served from Goonbarrow Junction.
- The Retew branch – From St Dennis Junction to Melangoose Mill; this was extended to Meledor Mill on 1 July 1912 and a further short extension to

Right: Pictured in May 1952, Newquay station sees two ex-GWR '4575' 2–6–2Ts awaiting departure: No 5519 on a service to Par and No 5562 with a train for Chacewater.
Ian Allan Library

New Meledor followed. Heavily used until the 1970s, the last working over the route was in April 1981 when a weed-killing train operated.

● Treloggan (Tolcarn) Junction-East Wheal Rose – This mineral line was subsequently extended to Treamble and thence, by reversal, to Gravel Hill. The section from Treamble to Gravel Hill was to close in 1888. The section from Tolcarn Junction to Shepherds was to become part of the GWR Newquay-Chacewater branch in 1905. The branch from Shepherds to Treamble closed originally on 1 January 1917, being quickly lifted; it was

Right: By the date of this photograph, 16 May 1969, Fowey station had been closed to passenger services for more than four years but the facilities remained almost as though a train was expected imminently. The only railway activity was, however, now the china clay traffic with a diesel shunter standing in the background awaiting its next duty.
W. A. Camwell

Left: This view taken in 1922 looking towards the south shows the extensive facilities provided at St Blazey Yard to deal with both china clay traffic and ordinary freight. On the right an 0-6-0PT can be seen shunting a rake of china clay wagons. In the centre can be seen the line heading south to Par Harbour and Fowey whilst to the left the line to the junction at Par with the main line can be identified heading off to the east. *Ian Allan Library*

relaid in 1925 and reopened on 16 February 1926. The final train operated over the line on 8 August 1949 with the official closure date being 1 January 1952. Part of the trackbed to the north of East Wheal Rose is now used by the 15in gauge Lappa Valley Railway following the closure of the Chacewater-Newquay line in 1963. At Treloggan Junction, a south-west curve was installed but this closed initially in 1888, being reinstated on 20 July 1931; final closure came on 28 October 1963 with the closure of the spur to Trevemper Siding.

- St Dennis-Drinnick Mill – Following the failure of the Newquay & Cornwall Junction Railway to complete its line north of Drinnick Mill, the CMR obtained powers to build the extension on 21 July 1873 – the same Act that empowered the CMR to take over the N&CJR – and the line was opened on 1 June 1874. The section from Parkandillack north to St Dennis Junction was closed on 6 February 1966. The southernmost section remains open and is served from the Burngullow end of the line.
- Goonbarrow branch – This freight-only line was opened on 2 October 1893 from Goonbarrow Junction to Gunheath and thence, following reversal, to Carbean. The section from New Caudeldown to Carbean closed on 3 December 1965 with the remainder, with the exception of sidings at Goonbarrow Junction, following in September 1973.

Culm Valley Light Railway

Authorised on 15 May 1873 as a light railway, using the provisions of the 1868 Regulation of Railways Act, and opened on 29 May 1876, the 7.25-mile long branch to Hemyock from Tiverton Junction failed to live up to the expectations of the line's promoters and the concern was sold to the GWR in April 1880. In 1910 there were four return workings per weekday with no Sunday services. Two intermediate stations – Uffculme and Culmstock – were provided. Passenger services over the line were withdrawn from the branch on

9 September 1963 but, courtesy of milk traffic, freight services over the line survived until October 1975.

Dartmouth & Torbay Railway

Authorised on 27 July 1957, this was an extension of the South Devon Railway route to Torre. The line opened to Paignton on 2 August 1859, to Brixham Road (later Churston) to 14 March 1861 (for passenger traffic; freight followed on 1 April 1861) and to Kingswear on 16 August 1864. Operated by the SDR from the outset, the line was leased by the larger concern in 1866 and completely absorbed six years later. The 6.75-mile long section of line from Paignton to Kingswear was closed completely with the withdrawal of passenger services on 30 October 1972 but was subsequently reopened by the Dart Valley Railway as the Paignton & Dartmouth Steam Railway with a its own station constructed alongside the BR one at Paignton.

Devon & Cornwall Railway

Originally promoted as the Okehampton Railway, the company became the D&CR on 26 July 1870. Backed by the LSWR and acquired by the larger company on 1 January 1872, the line was opened from North Tawton to Okehampton on 3 October 1871, thence to Lidford — the station was not renamed Lydford until 1897 — on 12 October 1874. The line was originally single track but was doubled by 1879. Passenger services over the line from Lydford to Okehampton ceased on 6 May 1968 at which date the section from Meldon Quarry to Lydford was to close completely. The line from Okehampton to Meldon remains open to serve the quarry at Meldon; today, the section from Coleford Junction to the quarry is in private ownership, It has also seen use by the Dartmoor Railway (see page 76). In 1873 powers were obtained for the construction of a line from Halwill Junction to Holsworthy (1865 powers for

Left: A Birmingham (Snow Hill) and Wolverhampton express is recorded pulling out of Kingswear station during the summer of 1953 behind 'Hall' class 4-6-0 No 4992 *Crosley Hall*. J. Lakin

Below: A decade later and much has changed at Kingswear in terms of traction with diesel power now well to the fore. On 4 September 1964 ,'Western' class No D1032 *Western Marksman* draws forward prior to running round its train having arrived at the head of the 09.35 service from Cardiff.
G. F. Gillham

Above: In March 1957 an unidentified ex-GWR '38xx' 2-8-0 heads towards Kingswear with a train of coal empties crossing Hookhill (Churston) Viaduct. *D. S. Fish*

Right: A busy scene at Paignton on 9 July 1973 sees two Class 50s in the station: No 50036 *Victorious* has just arrived with the 10.10 from Paddington whilst No 50032 *Courageous* waits to depart with the 14.05 service to Paddington. *Peter Marsh*

a line to Bude having expired); the eight-mile long section opened on 20 January 1879 (at the same time as the section from Meldon Junction to Halwill). This was to be the terminus of the line until the extension — with a replacement station at Holsworthy — to Bude opened in 1898. In April 1910 there were seven return workings over the line per weekday with a single return working on Sundays. A single journey over the section took about 16min. Passenger services were withdrawn over the line from Meldon Junction to Holsworthy on 3 October 1966, on which date the section was to close completely.

Left and below left:
Two views taken at Torquay looking in the down direction provide a fascinating contrast. The first, taken in April 1892, shows work in progress eliminating the broad gauge lines through the station. The second, taken 30 years later, in 1921, shows the extended platforms to the north, work undertaken shortly before the outbreak of World War 1. The middle line through the station, the Middle Siding, became disused from 14 April 1970 having lost its connection to the up line five years earlier. The station originally opened with the line to Paignton on 2 August 1859 with goods facilities being introduced two years later. *Ian Allan Library*

Devon & Cornwall Central Railway

Incorporated on 18 August 1882, the D&CCR was empowered to construct a link from Lydford to Callington; however, the project failed and the powers were transferred to the Plymouth, Devonport & South Western Junction Railway by an Act of 7 August 1884. The line south from Lydford was opened under the auspices of the PD&SWJR in 1890.

Devon & Somerset Railway

Authorised on 29 July 1864, the D&SR was a 42.25-mile long line that ran from Norton Fitzwarren to Barnstaple. The line opened in two stages: from Norton Fitzwarren to Wiveliscombe on 8 June 1871 and thence to Barnstaple on 1 November 1883. Originally constructed to broad gauge standards, the line

Right: Heading west from Taunton, the first of the intermediate stations on the branch towards Barnstaple in Devon was Venn Cross. On 22 August 1964 ex-GWR 2-6-0 No 7303 is pictured departing from the station with the 10.12am service from Ilfracombe. The coaches were combined with the stock from the 12.5pm service from Minehead at Taunton for onward travel to Paddington.
Michael J. Fox

Right: Although actually just in Somerset, Dulverton was the first intermediate station west of Morebath Junction on the line towards Barnstaple and is, therefore, perhaps better suited for inclusion here. On 22 June 1963 2-6-0 No 7326 is recorded departing from the station with the 1.57pm service from Taunton to Ilfracombe.
G. D. King

was operated from the outset by the Bristol & Exeter Railway. The line was converted to standard gauge in May 1881 and, on 1 June 1887 a connection – authorised on 31 August 1885 – with the LSWR route to Barnstaple was opened. This allowed the GWR access to the line to Ilfracombe. In 1910 there were five return workings per day with four continuing beyond Barnstaple to Ilfracombe. The journey time for a single trip from Taunton to Barnstaple was just under two hours. During the interwar years traffic over the route, particularly to Ilfracombe, increased with the result that the section from Norton Fitzwarren to Milverton was doubled in 1937. However, during the 1950s, railway economics turned against the line, particularly as traffic was

gradually diverted away from it or lost completely. The end came with the withdrawal of passenger services. All services had been concentrated on the ex-LSWR station with the closure of Barnstaple Victoria Road on 13 June 1960 but the entire route, despite dieselisation, was to see passenger services withdrawn on 3 October 1966. The final section of the line to close, the 1887-spur from the ex-LSWR line to Victoria Road station, came with the withdrawal of freight facilities from Victoria Road on 5 March 1970.

East Cornwall Mineral Railway

Originally incorporated as the Callington & Calstock Railway, being renamed the ECMR on 25 May 1871, this 3ft 6in line was authorised to provide a connection between mines and quarries in the Gunnislake and Kit Hill area with a quay on the River Tamar at Calstock. The line was opened throughout on 8 May 1872. Apart from a cable-worked incline plane at Calstock, the line was locomotive operated. Following an Act of 19 July 1887, the Plymouth, Devonport & South West Junction Railway took over on 1 June 1891. In 1900 the PD&SWJR obtained a Light Railway Order for the conversion of the line to standard gauge and, in 1905, its extension to Bere Alston. Passenger services over the line commenced on 2 March 1908. In 1910 there were four or five return workings from Bere Alston to Callington on weekdays with no Sunday service; the single journey for the 9.5-mile long trip took around 40min. Freight services along the Callington branch were withdrawn in February 1966 and the branch was closed completely between Gunnislake and Callington with the withdrawal of passenger services on 7 November 1966. The station at Gunnislake was relocated slightly to the east in January 1994.

Above: Two GWR coaches are recorded in the main platform at Barnstaple — later Barnstaple Victoria Road — station in this view looking towards the buffer stops. The station was originally opened by the Devon & Somerset Railway on 1 November 1873 as the terminus of the broad gauge line from Taunton. The line was converted to standard gauge eight years later. Passenger services continued to serve the terminus until 13 June 1960 when all remaining passenger services were concentrated on the ex-LSWR Junction station. The station was to close completely with the withdrawal of freight facilities a decade later. *Ian Allan Library*

Right: Cowley Bridge Junction was and remains the point at which the line towards Crediton and Barnstaple headed north off the ex-Bristol & Exeter main line towards Taunton. Here, on 23 September 1953, 'West Country' class No 34017 *Ilfracombe* passes over the junction with an up train heading towards Exeter St David's and Exeter Central. If the LSWR had ultimately obtained all the powers that it sought in the area, it would have constructed its own independent line from central Exeter to link with the line towards Barnstaple rather than relying on running powers over the GWR from St David's to Cowley Bridge Junction. The route towards Barnstaple has subsequently been singled and the bridge over the River Exe rebuilt. *C. F. H. Oldham*

Exeter & Crediton Railway

Although there had been an earlier scheme in 1832, it was not until 1 July 1845 that the Exeter & Crediton Railway obtained its powers to construct a 5.75-mile long line. Although only a relatively short route, the construction of the line and its opening were influenced by the controversy over gauge and by the desire of the LSWR, which had surreptitiously acquired shares in the company, to use the route as a means of gaining access to North Devon. The line was originally constructed as broad gauge but the LSWR prevented its opening – once a line had opened using one gauge a new Act of Parliament was required to change the gauge – and was thus converted to standard gauge with a proposed opening date of 15 February 1848. However, the Railway Commissioners decreed earlier in February that the associated Taw Valley Extension Railway should also be constructed as broad gauge with the result that the LSWR cancelled its proposed opening. Further delays resulted until the E&CR was leased to the Bristol & Exeter and, following reconversion to broad gauge, was opened throughout on 12 May 1851. The LSWR acquired the lease over the line on 1 February 1862 and, following an Act of 13 July 1876, converted the line to standard gauge (it had been mixed gauge from 1863). The LSWR formally acquired the ECR in 1879. The line remains open today as part of the branch from Cowley Bridge Junction to Barnstaple, with services provided by the First Great Western franchise.

Exeter & Exmouth Railway

Authorised on 2 July 1855, the Exeter & Exmouth Railway was the second scheme designed to provide a link to Exmouth and followed a proposal of 1846 that had failed. Initially authorised as a broad gauge line, the company was convinced by the LSWR to construct the line as a standard gauge branch in

Left: In 1976 the original terminus in Exmouth was closed and a new station constructed slightly to the north. On 10 April 1977 a DMU forming the 15.00 service from Exeter Central to Exmouth pulls into the relatively new station at Exmouth. The passenger accommodation provided was distinctly more Spartan than that provided previously.
Les Bertram

Left: On 14 July 1981 a Pressed Steel Class 117 DMU, with No W51373 leading, forms the 13.56 service from Exmouth to Exeter St Davids at Lympstone. The station was renamed Lympstone Village in 1991.
Brian Morrison

exchange for a share of Exeter Queen Street station. The line, which was opened throughout on 1 May 1861, had been leased by the LSWR on 6 August 1860 and was to be fully absorbed by the larger company on 1 January 1866. The line remains open for passenger services throughout with the exception of a slight shortening in Exmouth, where the station was relocated slightly to the north in 1976. Contemporary passenger services are provided by the First Great Western franchise.

Exeter Railway

Originally known as the Exeter, Teign Valley & Chagford Railway, the company became the Exeter Railway on 12 August 1898 with the abandonment of its

Right: The second
intermediate station on
the Exeter Railway branch
from Exeter St Thomas to
Christow was Longdown.
At 6.27pm on 11 June
1957, 0-6-0PT No 9765 is
pictured bringing the one-
coach service from Exeter
to Heathfield into
Longdown. Although a
useful diversionary route
for the ex-GWR main line
via Dawlish, passenger
services over the line
were to be withdrawn a
year later.
H. E. Fisher

plans for a branch to Chagford. Originally authorised in 1883, the line was not
to be opened from Exeter to Christow, where it met the earlier Teign Valley
Railway, until 1 July 1903. In 1910 there were eight return workings from
Exeter to Christow each weekday, with five running beyond Christow to
Heathfield. There was no service on Sundays. Apart from the local passenger
service, the route was also used as a diversionary line in the event of the main
line via Dawlish being closed. Passenger services over the line were withdrawn
on 9 June 1958, when the section from Christow to Exeter was closed
completely with the exception of a short section to Marsh Barton that
remained, and is still open, to serve a scrapyard.

Exeter, Teign Valley & Chagford Railway

This was authorised on 20 August 1883 to construct the 8.75-mile long line
from Christow to Exeter St Thomas and the 10-mile long branch to Chagford.
Although the first sod was cut in 1894, progress was slow and, following the
decision in 1898 to abandon the branch to Chagford, the company became the
Exeter Railway.

Exe Valley Railway

This was incorporated on 30 June 1874 to construct a line from Tiverton to
Stoke Canon on the Exeter-Bristol main line. Powers were later transferred to
the Bristol & Exeter in 1875 but the line was built by the GWR.

Great Western Railway

Although the majority of the GWR's network in the region was constructed by
earlier companies prior to being taken over by the GWR, a small number of
lines were opened under direct GWR control. These included:

- Bodmin Road to Bodmin General and Boscarne Junction – The LSWR-
  controlled Bodmin & Wenford was connected to the GWR main line
  courtesy of two short lines. The first section to open, from Bodmin Road

to Bodmin (GWR) was opened on 27 May 1887; this line was standard gauge from the outset. On 3 September 1888 the connection from Bodmin to Boscarne Junction was completed. Passenger services from Bodmin Road to Padstow ceased on 30 January 1967 although the china clay traffic from Wenford Bridge ensured that the line did not close completely until 18 November 1983. Following closure the line from Bodmin Road to Boscarne Junction was preserved as the Bodmin & Wenford Railway.

- GW (Millbay) Docks – Situated to the south of Plymouth Millbay station, the broad gauge connection to the docks first opened in 1850 to the South Devon Railway; the first standard gauge lines were laid in the mid-1870s. The line was extended to the East Wharf and Graving Dock in the late 1870s. The GWR and Western Region operated ocean specials from a terminal, which was last rebuilt in 1952, until late 1963. Rail-borne freight traffic over the branch ceased on 30 June 1971, at which point the line south from the ex-GWR main line past the closed Millbay station was also closed completely.

- North Quay branch – This was one of two freight-only branches ultimately to serve the North Quay in Plymouth and was opened on 6 November 1879. It was partially closed in 1969 with the remainder closing with the Sutton Harbour branch on 3 December 1973.

- Brent-Kingsbridge – The GWR took-over the Kingsbridge & Salcombe Railway in 1888; the line was, however, not opened until 19 December 1893. The 12.5-mile long branch, which was never completed to Salcombe a further six miles distant, saw six return workings per weekday in 1910 with one on Sundays. Both passenger and freight traffic over the branch were withdrawn on 16 September 1963.

- Tiverton-Stoke Canon – Originally authorised as the Exe Valley Railway in 1874, this 10.75-mile long branch was constructed by the GWR and opened on 1 August 1884. Linked with the line from Tiverton to Morebath Junction, the route had six return workings each weekday in 1910 with seven on Tuesdays. There was no service on Sundays. Passenger services over the line were withdrawn on 7 October 1963 on which date the line from Thorverton to Tiverton closed completely; the final section, from Stoke Canon to Thorverton, closed on 30 November 1966.

- Cornwall Loop – This short section of track, opened on 17 May 1876, formed the northernmost part of a triangular junction to the north of Plymouth Millbay station and was designed to allow LSWR trains to gain access to North Road station.

- Lipson Junction-Mount Gould Junction – This curve was opened on 1 April 1891 ultimately to permit LSWR passenger services to access the new station at Friary. The line remains operational, although no passenger services now use it.

- Friary Junction-Cattewater Junction – This short section of line, with one intermediate station (Mount Gould & Tothill Halt, open between 1905 and 1918), was opened on 17 January 1898 to permit GWR services to and from the Yealmpton branch to avoid reversal at Friary station. The line closed on 15 September 1958.

● Yealmpton branch — running from Plymstock on the LSWR line to Turnchapel, the 6.5-mile long GWR branch to Yealmpton opened on 17 January 1898. In April 1910 there were nine return workings per weekday with 10 on Saturdays and a Sunday service of three workings. Services ran to and from Millbay station and the single journey from

Right: In September 1946, during the six-year period when passenger services were restored to the Plymstock-Yealmpton branch, GWR 0-6-0PT No 6412 is pictured approaching the branch terminus.
B. A. Butt

Right: Plymstock was the junction for the LSWR branch to Turnchapel and the GWR branch towards Yealmpton. This view, taken in 1913 in the down direction, shows the GWR platform at Plymstock.
Ian Allan Library

Plymstock to Yealmpton took about 18min. Passenger services over the Yealmpton branch were withdrawn initially on 7 July 1930 but were reinstated as a wartime measure on 3 November 1941 to Friary; unadvertised workmen's services had commenced on the preceding 21 July. Passenger services were again withdrawn on 6 October 1947 and completely on 29 February 1960.

- Chacewater-Newquay – The first section of the branch, from Chacewater to Perranporth – opened on 6 July 1903 and the line reached Newquay on 2 January 1905. The section from Shepherds to Tolcarn Junction at Newquay was constructed over the line of the existing mineral branch to East Wheal Rose. In April 1910 there were six return workings per weekday with an additional late train on Saturdays; there was no Sunday service. A single journey over the 18.5-mile long route between Chacewater and Newquay took around 53min from Chacewater and just over an hour in the reverse direction. Initially, there was a triangular junction at Chacewater but this was simplified in 1924 to a parallel track running into Chacewater station. Passenger services over the route were withdrawn on 4 February 1963, on which date the line between Chacewater and Trevemper Siding, one mile from Tolcarn Junction, was to close completely. The final section closed on 28 October 1963. A short section of the line north of East Wheal Rose mine is now operated as the 15in gauge Lappa Light Railway.
- Trenance Valley – The freight-only branch from Trenance Junction, near St Austell, to Lansalson opened to Bojea Sidings on 1 May 1920 and throughout on 24 May 1920. It closed north of Boskell Sidings on 27 July with the remainder succumbing on 6 May 1968.

Hayle Railway

Authorised as a standard gauge line on 27 June 1834, the Hayle Railway was empowered to construct a main line between Hayle and Tresaveen (Gwenna),

Left: The first intermediate station north of Chacewater was Mount Hawke Halt. The halt, with its standard GWR pagoda shelter, opened in August 1905 some two years after the opening of the section from Chacewater to Perranporth. 2-6-2T No 5562, heads through the station with a freight bound for Truro.
G. Clarke

31

Right: On 20 May 1959, '45xx' 2-6-2T No 5519 is pictured at Chacewater station awaiting departure with the 1.35pm service to Newquay.
M. Mensing

a distance of some 12 miles, with an additional five miles of branch line. The first section to open was the branch to Portreath on 23 December 1837. There were four inclined planes — at Angarrack, Penponds, Redruth and Portreath Harbour — with locomotives being used on the remainder of the route except at Hayle, initially, and Portreath. The section from Carn Brae Mines to Redruth opened for goods traffic on 11 June 1838. Other branches were opened to Hayle wharves, Crofty and Roskear mines and Redruth. From 23 May 1843 a passenger service from Redruth to Hayle was operated. In 1846 the West Cornwall Railway was authorised to rebuild the Hayle Railway and extend it to Truro and Penzance. Under the WCR, which formally took over the Hayle Railway on 3 December 1846, the line was converted to broad gauge and the line diverted to avoid the inclined planes at Angarrack and Penponds.

Haytor Tramway

At the end of the 18th century, the Stover Canal was constructed to transport ball clay from Teigngrace to the Teign estuary. On 16 September 1820, the Haytor Tramway was opened to provide a feeder to the canal from the local granite quarries. The line, which was built to a gauge of 4ft 3in, was constructed from granite and represented the first railway constructed in Devon. It extended for some six miles, rising 1,200ft. The line continued to function until the 1850s and its remains are now a scheduled ancient monument. Part of the tramway's trackbed, between Teigngrace and Bovey Tracey, was used for the Moretonhampstead & South Devon Railway, which opened on 4 July 1866.

Left: Viewed from the north on 10 June 1920, this view of Helston station shows, in the foreground, the one-road engine shed. In the distance can be seen the carriage shed that was to be demolished in the late 1950s.
Ian Allan Library

Helston Railway

Authorised on 9 July 1880, the 8.75-mile long branch from Gwinear Road to Helston opened on 9 May 1887. A Light Railway Order was subsequently granted for an extension to The Lizard; in the event, this was never constructed and, in its place, the GWR launched its first bus service on 17 August 1903. In 1910, there were nine return workings per weekday over the branch with two on Sundays. The single journey took between 25 and 29min. Passenger services over the branch were withdrawn on 5 November 1962 but the line was not to close completely until the withdrawal of freight facilities on 5 October 1964. A small preservation scheme has been established near Trevano Gardens.

Left: There were three advertised intermediate stations between Helston and Gwinear Road; the northernmost of the trio was that at Praze. This view shows the station looking towards the north. There was a loop at the station until 1938 when the connection at the southern end was disconnected and the loop converted into a siding.
Ian Allan Library

Right: Recorded on 17 July 1956, this view of Brent station sees 0-6-0PT No 3796 at the head of a branch train to Kingsbridge whilst 'Hall' class 4-6-0 No 4998 *Eyton Hall* heads the 7.55am service from Penzance to Swansea.
R. J. Doran

Right : Gara Bridge was the principal intermediate station between Brent and Kingsbridge. It opened with the line on 19 December 1893. This view, taken looking in the down direction towards Kingsbridge, shows the main station building. Of the three intermediate stations on the branch, Gara Bridge was the only one to possess a signalbox, which was located at the Brent end of the up platform, behind the photographer.
N. L. M. Stone

Right : A general view of the terminus of the 12.5-mile long branch at Kingsbridge taken on 9 February 1955 showing the goods yard, station platforms and locomotive shed.
P. C. Sambourne

Kingsbridge & Salcombe Railway

Backed by the GWR, the K&SR was incorporated on 24 July 1882 to assume the powers authorised by an Act of 29 May 1864 to the Kingsbridge Railway for the construction of a branch from Brent on the SDR main line. The company was absorbed by the GWR on 13 August 1888 before the line was opened.

Launceston & South Devon Railway

This 19-mile line, from Launceston to Tavistock, was authorised on 30 June 1862 and opened to freight traffic throughout on 1 June 1865. Passenger services were introduced on 1 July the same year. The line was operated by the South Devon Railway from the outset and was taken over by the larger railway following an Act of 24 June 1869. In 1910 there were four return workings per weekday, five on Saturdays, with a solitary service on Sundays. A single journey took around 45min. In 1943, during World War 2, a connection between the GWR and SR lines at Launceston was constructed; after Nationalisation this enabled all passenger services to be concentrated on the ex-SR station with the closure of the ex-GWR Launceston station on 30 June 1952. Passenger services from Launceston South to Tavistock were withdrawn on 31 December 1962, with the sections between Marsh Mills and Tavistock South and between Lifton and Launceston closing completely on the same day. The latter section reopened on 7 September 1964 with the withdrawal of freight traffic over the North Cornwall line. The section south from Lydford to Tavistock South closed completely on 25 September 1964 whilst the final closure, from Lydford to Launceston came on 28 February 1966.

Launceston, Bodmin & Wadebridge Junction Railway

This line was incorporated on 29 July 1864 to construct a line from Launceston to a junction with the Bodmin & Wadebridge Railway as well as a branch to

Left: On 16 April 1960, ex-GWR 2-6-2T No 4549 arrives at Tavistock South station with the 12.40pm (Saturdays Only) service from Launceston to Plymouth. Note that the locomotive has lost its smokebox number and simply has its number painted in bright yellow shaded with dark brown on the buffer beam. *J. C. Haydon*

Ruthern Bridge; with the abandonment of the branch, the company changed its name to the Cornwall Central Railway.

Lee Moor Tramway

The original powers to construct the future Lee Moor Tramway were granted to the Devon & Tavistock Railway on 24 July 1854. The line, ultimately built to the 4ft 6in gauge, was poorly built and, following its opening in September the same year, was to close on 4 October 1854 following an accident at Torycombe, one of two inclined plans on the line (the other was at Cann). By the time that the line was reopened on 24 September 1858, ownership had passed to Lord Morley, over whose land the line mostly passed. The line was extended beyond Lee Moor to Cholwich Town at the same time; this section was to close c1910. The line used both horse and steam power away from the inclined planes. The section from Torycombe Incline to Lee Moor Village was

Right: The last section of the Lee Moor Tramway to remain operational was that which crossed the ex-GWR main line on the level just to the east of Laira Junction. This section closed in 1960 and this view records the scene at the crossing shortly afterwards, with the main line now plain track but with evidence of the crossing clearly shown in the foreground.
Ian Allan Library

Right: The 4ft 6in gauge Lee Moor Tramway possessed two steam locomotives, both of which were 0-4-0STs built by Peckett & Sons of Bristol in 1899. This view shows No 2; the two locomotives always faced in the Cann Wood direction. After a long career eventually culminating with English China Clays, both of the ex-Lee Moor locomotives survive in preservation.
Ian Allan Library

Left: The Liskeard & Caradon Railway operated using both horse and locomotive power; 0-6-0T *Caradon* was supplied to the railway in 1862.
Ian Allan Library

closed in 1936; that between Marsh Mills and the Cann Wood Incline in 1955. The final section, from Laira to Marsh Mills, which was latterly horse operated and which crossed the ex-GWR main line on the level just to the east of Laira Junction, was closed in the autumn of 1960 and lifted over the following two years.

Liskeard & Caradon Railway

Following the opening of the Liskeard & Looe Union Canal in the late 1820s, the Liskeard & Caradon Railway was incorporated on 27 June 1843 to provide a standard gauge link between the canal and the quarries and mines to the north of Liskeard. The first section, from Moorswater to South Caradon, opened on 28 November and the line was extended to Cheesewring Quarry, via the Gonamena incline, in March 1846. A branch from South Caradon to Tokenbury Corner was opened in 1861 to be followed by a line in 1869 from Minions to Phoenix Mine and, in August 1877, a further branch from Tokenbury to Marke Valle Mine. In 1882, the Tokenbury branch was extended round to Cheesewring, allowing for the closure of the Gonamena incline. To the north of Cheesewring, the Kilmar Railway provided a link to quarries at North Kilmar, Kilmar Tor and Bearah, although this only operated from 1858 to 1877. In 1883 the Kilmar line was temporarily resurrected in connection with a proposed extension, on which work started, towards the LSWR at Launceston. In 1901, the Liskeard & Looe Railway, which had been previously leased by the L&CR, acquired a lease over the L&CR. This was to continue until 1 July 1909 when the GWR took over the L&CR. All of the L&CR's operations north of Moorswater were abandoned on 31 January 1916 with the line being rapidly dismantled for use in the war effort.

Liskeard & Looe Railway

In order to aid the exploitation of the minerals from which the area derived much of its wealth, the Liskeard & Looe Union Canal was authorised by an Act

Right: At Liskeard, the branch line trains for Looe depart from a platform that is set at a right angle to main line, on the up side, with trains making a sharp turn to the east before passing under the main line en route to Coombe Junction. On 23 July 1965 a Gloucester RC&W single-unit waits at the platform at Liskeard with a service to Looe.
R. Maundrell

Right: A Gloucester RC&W single-unit stands at the station in Looe on 15 October 1965. The line was originally extended beyond the station but, by the date of this photograph, freight services over the branch had been withdrawn.
D. W. J. Bartlett

of 22 June 1825 to construct a canal between the two settlements. The canal was to open progressively between 1826 and 1828. Over the next three decades traffic grew rapidly and, by an Act of 11 May 1858, the canal company was empowered to construct a railway line from Looe to connect with the existing Liskeard & Caradon Railway. The line was opened throughout on 27 December 1860. Initially designed for freight traffic only, pressure for the provision of a passenger service resulted in the necessary works eventually being undertaken and, on 11 September 1879 passenger services were introduced. Originally, there was only one intermediate station – Causeland – but this was closed between 1881, when Sandplace station opened, and 1888. Initially, the passenger service was divorced from the main railway network

Left: Viewed across the river, GWR 0-6-0ST No 1941 stands at Looe station on 10 July 1924 at the head of service to Liskeard.
H. C. Casserley

but, in 1895, powers were obtained, as the Liskeard & Looe Junction Railway, to construct a connection from Coombe Junction to Liskeard. This two-mile section of line was opened on 25 February 1901 for freight traffic and the following 8 May for passenger trains. Following the GWR's takeover of the Liskeard & Caradon, the larger company took over operation of the Looe branch on 1 July 1909 although the L&LR remained independent until the Grouping in 1923. In April 1910 there were seven down workings (eight on Saturdays and two on Sundays) per weekday with six up workings (except on Mondays and Saturdays when there were seven and one on Sundays). The average journey time for the single 8.75-mile long trip was about 30min. The current franchisee of the branch to Looe is First Great Western.

London & South Western Railway

The LSWR was one of the two dominant pre-Grouping railway companies in the region. Although it took over a number of lines in building its local network, it also directly sponsored the construction of a small number of lines in Devon and Cornwall. These included:

- Yeovil-Exeter – Although initially there were two possibilities for a standard gauge connection to Exeter – either via the coast or via a central route through Salisbury – it was the latter that ultimately found favour. On 21 July 1856 the LSWR obtained powers to construct an extension from Yeovil – where it met the already approved Salisbury & Yeovil Railway – with the line opening throughout on 19 July 1860 to a new terminus at Exeter Queen Street. On 3 July 1860 the LSWR obtained powers to extend the line through to Exeter St David's and to construct mixed gauge lines through the station, on to Cowley Bridge Junction and over the lines north of there to Bideford. The short, but steeply graded connection, opened on 1 February 1862 at the same time as the mixed gauge line through to

Cowley Bridge Junction. The line remains open throughout with passenger services today provided by the South West Trains franchise.

- Plymouth Friary — Initially LSWR operated services to Plymouth North Road, which was jointly controlled with the GWR, but on 1 July 1891 it opened its own four-platform terminus. The route followed was over the freight-only branch from Friary Junction, on the Sutton Harbour line, which had opened on 1 February 1878. Passenger services were withdrawn from Plymouth Friary on 15 September 1958 although freight facilities

Right: Axminster station is the first station in Devon to be met by passengers travelling over the Yeovil-Exeter line. This view, taken looking towards the west in September 1962, sees Ivatt 2-6-2T No 41322 departing with a branch-line service to Lyme Regis with the main line to its left. The departing service will initially curve to the right, then cross over the main line slightly to the west of the station before heading to the Dorset coast.
Ian Allan Library

Right: A three-car DMU departs from Exeter Central on 14 September 1976 with the 07.58 service from Exeter St David's to Exmouth.
L. Bertram

continued to be provided. There is still rail activity at Friary, with sidings providing access to the remains of the Cattewater branch.

- North Quay branch — Opened on 22 October 1879, this short branch in Plymouth was to close in November 1950 as it duplicated an ex-GWR route.
- Stonehouse Pool branch — Opened in 1876 and 1877, this line diverged from the Plymouth, Devonport & South West Junction Railway to the east of Kings Road station. The LSWR operated an Ocean terminal at the southernmost end of the branch between 9 April 1904 and 1911. Freight traffic over the Stonehouse Pool branch ceased in the mid-1960s and the line was officially closed on 7 March 1971.
- Cattewater branch — Notionally built under the auspices of the Plymouth & Dartmoor Railway, the first section of this freight-only branch was opened on 3 August 1880. It was extended to its final terminus eight years later. The line remains operational serving a bitumen works.
- Turnchapel branch — Again notionally built under the auspices of the P&DR, as agent for the LSWR, the line had opened as far as Plymstock with the completion of the Laira Bridge on 5 September 1892. The line was extended to Turnchapel on 1 January 1897. The line extended a further half-mile beyond the branch terminus to serve an Admiralty site. In April 1910 the 2.5-mile long route from Plymouth Friary saw 23 return workings per week day (of which two operated only as far as Plymstock); the single journey between Plymouth and Turnchapel took 10min. Passenger services were suspended in early 1951 before being withdrawn completely on 10 September 1951. The line between Plymstock and Turnchapel was to close completely on 26 October that year. Thereafter, until closure on 14 September 1987, the line from Turnchapel Branch Junction to Plymstock across the Laira Bridge remained open for cement traffic.
- Bude-Holsworthy — Earlier powers to construct a line to Bude had lapsed

Left: On 10 August 1984, Class 08 No 08792 pulls some oil tanks along the Cattewater branch towards Plymouth Friary. This is now the only remaining section of a once extensive network of lines that served the docks and industrial sites in east Plymouth.
Rod Muncey

Right: Ivatt 2-6-2T No 41313 — which was later to be preserved — is pictured awaiting departure from Bude station with a two-coach train.
Ian Allan Library

with the result that the LSWR promoted its own extension. The 10.5-mile long extension from Holsworthy opened on 10 August 1898. Amongst the civil engineering was the 500ft-long Holsworthy Viaduct; this was one of the first railway viaducts ever constructed in concrete. In April 1910 there were seven down workings from Holsworthy on weekdays with one on Sundays; there were eight up workings with again one on Sundays. A single journey over the section was timed at 19min in the down direction and about 22min in the up. Passenger services to Bude were withdrawn on 3 October 1966 when the entire section from Halwill Junction closed completely.

● Budleigh Salterton-Exmouth – Following the LSWR's working agreement with the Budleigh Salterton Railway, the LSWR promoted an extension of the existing line from Budleigh Salterton to Exmouth. This 4.75-mile long

Right: Viewed looking towards Lostwithiel, Class 14xx 0-4-2T No 1419 is recorded here, on a May day in 1950, departing from Fowey with a single-coach service to Lostwithiel. Heading towards the station is 2-8-0 No 4298 at the head of a train of empty china clay wagons destined for St Blazey.
B. A. Butt

extension opened on 1 June 1903. Passenger services were withdrawn over the line were withdrawn on 6 March 1967 on which date the line was to close completely.

Lostwithiel & Fowey Railway

Incorporated on 30 June 1862, the Lostwithiel & Fowey Railway was empowered to construct a broad gauge branch to Carne Point, one mile short of Fowey, predominantly for the movement of china clay. The line opened throughout on 1 June 1869 but was to struggle financially in competition with the Cornwall Minerals Railway and was forced to close on 1 January 1880. The assets of the company were transferred to the CMR following an Act of 27 June 1892 and was reopened as a standard gauge line, linked to the existing branch to Fowey from St Blazey, by the GWR (who had acquired the CMR) on 16 September 1895. In April 1910 there were five return workings per day between Lostwithiel and Fowey on weekdays but no service on Sundays. A single journey over the 5.25-mile long branch with one intermediate stop at Golant took 15min. Although passenger services over the line were suspended on four occasions — once during World War 1 and thrice during World War 2 — the service was to survive until 4 January 1965. The line remains open for china clay traffic to the harbour at Fowey.

Lynton & Barnstaple Railway

After the failure of earlier schemes, the 1ft 11.5in Lynton & Barnstaple Railway was promoted by the local population to provide a link with the standard gauge network at Barnstaple. Authorised on 27 June 1895, the 19.5-mile long line opened throughout on 11 May 1898 officially and to the public five days later. The line was operated independently until the Grouping in 1923, although negotiations had commenced with the LSWR for a takeover in 1922 following a decline in the railway's finances. In 1910 there were three return workings per weekday with five on Fridays; there was one return working on Sundays.

Left: Two of the Lynton & Barnstaple 2-6-2Ts, Nos 759 *Yeo* and 761 *Taw*, are pictured at Pilton shortly before the line's closure. The line's three original locomotives were built by Manning Wardle in Leeds.
A. B. MacLeod/ Ian Allan Library

Right: Following the first three locomotives, the Lynton & Barnstaple's next locomotive — *Lyn* — was acquired from Baldwin in the USA in 1900. Assembled at Pilton, the 2-4-2T was placed in traffic after clearance problems with its whistle were resolved. The locomotive is seen here in 1934. The line's final locomotive was another Manning Wardle example, a 2-6-2T delivered in 1925 and named *Lew*.
A. B. MacLeod/ Ian Allan Library

The journey time for a single journey was around 90min. The SR continued to operate the L&BR until the last service ran on 29 September 1935. Following closure, the line was dismantled. With interest in railway preservation growing, a scheme for the partial restoration of the line was established at Woody Bay in 1995 with limited services commencing in 2004.

Marland Light Railway

Opened in 1880, this private 3ft 0in gauge line ran south from Torrington, where it connected with the Bideford Extension Railway, to the North Devon Clay Co's works at Marland. The line survived until 1922–25 when the five-mile section from Torrington southwards was converted to standard gauge as part of the North Devon & Cornwall Junction Light Railway. The 3ft 0in gauge was retained within the works and the last clay to depart by rail left Marland in 1968.

Right: The Marland Light Railway was originally constructed to 3ft gauge in order to transport china clay from workings on Merton and Marland moors to Torrington. The bulk of the line was converted to standard gauge in the early 1920s with the construction of the line from Torrington to Halwill Junction. This is one of the Marland Light Railway's 0-6-0Ts, No 2 *Marland*, built by Bagnall in 1883 and delivered new to the railway. The locomotive was to survive until it was scrapped in 1925. *Ian Allan Library*

Mineral and Miscellaneous Lines

In addition to the railways otherwise featured in this book, Devon and Cornwall also possessed a umber of industrial and minor lines. Some of the major lines are covered elsewhere, but the following also merit attention:

- Bullpoint Government Sidings – Sited to the west of the ex-GWR main line at St Budeaux, this short line opened on 2 June 1916. Traffic continued until the late 1980s but ceased by about 1990.
- Plymouth Dockyard Railway – Diverging from the GWR main line to the north of Keyham, the Dockyard Railway opened in 1867 and included a 976yd-long tunnel. Between 1900 and 16 May 1966 an internal passenger service linking six stations was operated. Internal freight traffic ceased on 10 November 1982. The line from Keyham to the exchange sidings remains operational.
- Sutton Harbour – Opened in May 1853, this line, originally constructed to 4ft 6in (Dartmoor) gauge, was subsequently additionally fitted with broad gauge track for use by the South Devon Railway and provided access from Laira to Sutton Harbour in Plymouth. Ultimately, following the introduction of locomotives, broad and Dartmoor gauge tracks ran parallel. A branch, constructed by the GWR, headed off the Sutton Harbour branch to serve North Quay. Traffic to Sutton Harbour ceased on 18 December 1972 and the remains of the branch were closed completely beyond Friary Junction on 3 December 1973.
- Zeal Tor Tramway – A short-lived 3.5-mile long line opened in 1847 to transport peat from a site near Redlake to a naphtha works at Shipley Bridge.

Moretonhampstead & South Devon Railway

Authorised on 7 July 1862, this 12.5-mile long broad gauge branch from Newton Abbot to Moretonhampstead opened throughout on 4 July 1866. The line was

Left: Bovey station was the first intermediate station on the Moretonhampstead line north of the Teign Valley line at Heathfield until the opening of Brimley Halt in 1928. This view, taken on 28 February 1959 looking towards Moretonhampstead, illustrates well the facilities provided at the station. Normal practice was to use the right hand of the two platforms unless two trains were passing in the station and so starting signals, visible at the platform ends, were provided on both lines.
M. Windeatt

operated from the outset by the South Devon Railway and absorbed by the larger company following an Act of 18 July 1872. In 1910 there were five return workings per weekday with six on Wednesdays, Saturdays and the fourth Friday of each month; there were two return workings on Sundays. The journey time for a single journey was 44min in the down direction and 35min in the up. At Moretonhampstead there was a bus connection for Chagford; this had commenced operation in 1906. During the interwar period the line was popular with holidaymakers, but this traffic did not revive after 1945. Passenger services were withdrawn on 2 March 1959. The section from Bovey to Moretonhampstead closed completely on 6 April 1964 and that between Heathfield and Bovey Tracey on 4 May 1970 (although a final passenger service ran on 6 July 1970). The section from Newton Abbot to Heathfield remains open for freight traffic.

Newquay & Cornwall Junction Railway

Authorised on 14 July 1864, the Newquay & Cornwall Junction Railway was empowered to construct a broad gauge line of 5 miles 13 chains in length from Burngullow to connect with the Cornwall Minerals Railway at Hendra. The three-mile section from Burngullow to Drinnick Mill opened on 1 July 1869 but the cost of the original section allied to over-optimistic traffic projections meant that the extension to Hendra was not completed. On 21 July 1873 the CMR obtained powers to construct this section as a standard gauge line and lay mixed gauge track southwards, although the latter requirement was never complied with. The Cornwall Railway tried to enforce this clause, with the result that the CMR laid a third — but unusable — line and it was not until 1892, with the conversion of the broad gauge, that through running was possible. The N&CJR became part of the CMR following the 1873 Act. On 16 December 1909, following a court case, a 20-chain section at Carpella was removed to permit the extraction of china clay; it was not until 18 April 1922 that the GWR

Left: Ex-LSWR Class T9 4-4-0 No 30712 recorded departing from Padstow. To the right of the locomotive is the servicing area, with turntable. This was first established by the LSWR to the east of the station in 1900. The turntable was relocated further south in 1933 and enlarged, after World War 2, to accommodate the Bulleid Pacifics. The turntable ceased to be used in the early 1960s.
B. A Butt

opened a deviation route to reconnect the two sections of track. The line from Burngullow to Drinnick Mill remains open for the use of china clay traffic.

North Cornwall Railway

Emerging on 18 August 1882 from the Central Cornwall Railway, the NCR was empowered to construct the line from Halwill Junction to Wadebridge. The first section of the line to open was that from Halwill to Launceston, which was opened on 21 July 1886. This was followed by that from Launceston to

Above: Otterham was one of seven intermediate stations between Wadebridge and Launceston. The station was recorded here in September 1959 as Class T9 4-4-0 heads a train from Padstow to Exeter. *Derek Cross*

Right: It's August 1953 and, by this date, all passenger services in Launceston had been concentrated on the ex-LSWR South station with the closure the previous year of the ex-GWR North. Here an ex-GWR 2-6-2T, No 4591, is recorded in Launceston station with a service from Plymouth.
Ian Allan Library

Tresmeer on 28 July 1892, Tresmeer-Camelford on 14 August 1893, Camelford-Delabole on 18 October 1893 and thence to Wadebridge on 1 June 1895. The extension from Wadebridge to Padstow opened on 27 March 1899. Nominally independent, the NCR was worked from the outset by the LSWR. A single journey over the 49.75-mile route from Halwill Junction to Wadebridge took 90min in April 1910. The line was of prime importance during the summer but by the early 1960s rationalisation was to the fore. Through carriages to and from Waterloo were withdrawn on 5 September 1964 and freight traffic over the route ceased the following year. Steam was replaced by diesel traction

Right: The second intermediate station south of Torrington on the line to Halwill Junction was Petrockstow.
On 14 October 1969, North British-built diesel-hydraulic No D6334, having propelled seven wagons and a brake van from Meeth, has just run round its train prior to heading north towards Torrington. By this date the section south from Meeth to Halwill Junction had been lifted. The section south from Torrington was to last until the early 1980s.
Ian Allan Library

Left: Hatherleigh station viewed in 1931 only six years after the opening of the line.
Ian Allan Library

Right: The next intermediate station on the North Devon & Cornwall Junction Railway after Hatherleigh was Hole. This view, looking in the down direction towards Halwill Junction, dates from 1931.
Ian Allan Library

Left: In July 1964, Ivatt 2-6-2T No 41248 was recorded at Halwill with a one-coach Torrington train. Passenger services over the line to Torrington would be withdrawn the following year.
Ian Allan Library

for the remaining passenger services on 3 January 1965. Passenger services between Halwill Junction and Wadebridge were withdrawn on 3 October 1966 on which date the line was to close completely.

North Devon & Cornwall Junction Light Railway

Constructed by the light railway 'King', Colonel Holman F. Stephens, the 20.5-mile long line from Torrington to Halwill Junction was originally incorporated on 28 August 1914 — not an ideal date from the point of view of constructing a new railway — and as a result of World War 1, powers had to be renewed on 22 April 1922. Work started on the line's construction on 30 June 1922 and the line was opened throughout on 27 July 1925. Although operated from the outset by the Southern Railway, the ND&CJLR remained independent until Nationalisation. Passenger services over the line were withdrawn on 1 March 1965, at which stage the section of line between Meeth and Halwill Junction closed completely, although the final train — a special — did not operate until 27 March 1965. The section from Meeth to Torrington was formally closed from 8 November 1982. The trackbed of the line has been incorporated into a cycleway.

North Devon Railway & Dock Co

Renamed from the Taw Vale Railway & Dock Co (incorporated in 1838), the NDR&D was authorised to construct a three-mile line from Barnstaple to Fremington and to construct a quay at the latter site by an Act of 24 July 1851. The broad gauge line — it had originally been constructed as standard gauge as part of the LSWR's machinations but had been converted prior to opening — was opened on 12 July 1854 but services did not commence officially until 1 August 1854. The line was initially leased by the Bristol & Exeter and then by Thomas Brassey, who also leased the Bideford Extension Railway, before

Right: Recorded on 17 June 1959, ex-LSWR 'O2' class 0-4-4T No 30183 is pictured at the branch terminus of Callington at the head of a short mixed train for the journey back towards Plymouth. This particular 'O2' was built in May 1890 and was to last in service until September 1961.
G. M. Kichenside

the LSWR took over the lease on 1 January 1863. The line was quickly converted to mixed gauge in order to permit the first standard gauge train from Barnstaple to Bideford on 1 March 1863. The NDR&D was absorbed by the LSWR on 1 January 1865. In April 1910, Fremington was served by trains between Torrington and Barnstaple, with nine workings each weekday and two on Sundays. Trains were permitted five minutes between Fremington and Barnstaple. Passenger services ceased between Barnstaple Junction and Torrington on 4 October 1965 although the line remained open for freight traffic thereafter until complete closure on 5 March 1983.

Okehampton Railway

Incorporated on 17 July 1862, the Okehampton Railway represented an attempt to construct a standard gauge route through central Devon. The line originally authorised stretched from Coleford Junction to Okehampton; however, further powers were obtained on 13 July 1863 for the construction of an extension to Lydford – then called Lidford – on the broad gauge Launceston & South Devon Railway and for a third rail to be added to the broad gauge line from there to Plymouth. A further act of 29 June 1865 empowered the railway to construct a further 41 miles from Meldon Junction to Bude. Prior to the company changing its name, on 26 July 1870, to the Devon & Cornwall Railway, only two sections of line had opened: from Coleford Junction to North Tawton on 1 November 1865 and thence to Okehampton Road (later Belstone Corner) on 8 January 1867. The route represented the LSWR/SR main line from Exeter to Plymouth; passenger services were withdrawn from Okehampton to Coleford Junction on 5 June 1972 although the line remained open thereafter to access the quarry at Meldon. Limited summer seasonal passenger services have operated to recent years to Okehampton.

Pentewan Railway

This 2ft 6in gauge line extended for some four miles from quarries around St Austell to a harbour on the St Austell River at Pentewan. Engineered by Richard Carveth, the line opened in June 1829 and was operated partly by gravity and partly by horse. Following an Act of 1874, which allowed for the creation of the St Austell & Pentewan Railway, Harbour & Dock Co on 7 August of that year, locomotive power arrived on the line. However, silting of the harbour along with the growth of Par and Fowey led to the decline of the quay and the last train was to operate on 29 January 1918. Although the line was dismantled for the war effort, this was not quite the end of the story as a 2ft 6in-gauge tramway operated by the Pentewan Dock & Concrete Co ran along part of the trackbed between 1938 and 1966.

Plymouth & Dartmoor Railway

Promoted by Sir Thomas Tyrwhitt as a means of further developing Dartmoor, the P&DR was authorised on 2 July 1819 to construct a railway from Crabtree on the Plym estuary to Princetown, where he had been instrumental in getting a prison built. Tyrwhitt anticipated the traffic for the line would include granite from King Tor and Dartmoor peat. A second act, dated 8 July 1820, allowed for an extension from Crabtree to Sutton Pool with a branch to Cattewater. The 23-mile long line from Sutton Pool to King Tor, constructed to a gauge of 4ft 6in, opened on 26 September 1823. The line was, however, not a success financially and was for many years effectively controlled by John and William Johnson, who were quarry owners. Following refinancing in 1865, the line was relaid. The section beyond Yelverton was eventually taken over by the standard gauge Princetown Railway and the section between Marsh Mills and Laira by the South Devon Railway. The Lee Moor Tramway absorbed the section from the Rising Sun to Plymouth. The remainder of the route saw limited traffic until c1900 with the track being lifted in 1916.

Plymouth, Devonport & South Western Junction Railway

Incorporated on 25 August 1883, the PD&SWJR was authorised to construct a 22.5-mile long line from Devonport to Lydford. The double-track route, operated from the outset by the LSWR, opened on 2 June 1890. The PD&SWJR took over the East Cornwall Mineral Railway on 1 June 1891 and obtained powers in 1900 to convert the narrow gauge line to standard gauge. The line from Calstock to Callington, an extension of the PD&SWJR-controlled Bere Alston & Calstock Railway, opened on 2 March 1908. The PD&SWJR operated the line from Bere Alston to Callington itself, remaining independent of the LSWR until 1922. During World War 2 a connection between the GW and SR lines was constructed at St Budeaux; this connection allowed for the section of the original PD&SWJR line between Devonport Junction and St Budeaux to be closed completely on 7 September 1964 with passenger services being diverted to operate over the ex-GW main line and then via the wartime spur to St Budeaux Victoria Road. The ex-PD&SWJ main line, from Bere Alston to Lydford, closed completely on 6 May 1968 with the withdrawal of passenger

Right: The branch terminus at Callington viewed on 7 April 1953 sees 'O2' class 0-4-4T No 30236 awaiting departure with the 1pm service for Bere Alston.
R. E. Vincent

Left: In August 1953, 'O2' 0-4-4T No 30199 awaits departure from Bere Alston with a service for Callington.
Ian Allan Library

Left: On 28 June 1982, a three-car DMU departs from Bere Ferrers with the 08.12 service to Plymouth. This section of the Plymouth, Devonport & South West Junction main line is now singled and forms part of the surviving branch between Plymouth and Gunnislake.
C. R. D. Hack

services between Bere Alston and Okehampton. Today, passenger services operate between Plymouth and Gunnislake with the current franchisee being First Great Western.

Poldice Tramway

The earliest line in Cornwall, construction of this line was started on 29 October 1809 to provide a link between the harbour at Portreath primarily to ship minerals, in particular copper from Poldice, although limited passenger traffic was also catered for. The exact opening date is uncertain, although it was operational by 1812. The main copper mines at Poldice became exhausted by the mid-1850s although other mines continued to provide traffic. However, the line seems to have gone out of use by the mid-1860s although it was not finally dismantled until the early 20th century.

Princetown Railway

A subsidiary of the Great Western Railway, the Princetown Railway was authorised to construct a 10.5-mile long branch from Yelverton to Princetown on 13 August 1878. Part of the narrow-gauge line was constructed on the trackbed of the erstwhile Plymouth & Dartmoor Railway, acquired for £22,000, and the line was opened throughout on 11 August 1883. In 1910 there were six down workings on weekdays with an additional departure on Saturdays; there was one down working on Sundays. In the up direction there were five workings on weekdays, except for Tuesday when there were four and Saturdays when there were seven. There was one was one up working on Sunday. The majority of journeys ran beyond Yelverton to and from Plymouth. The journey time from Yelverton to Princetown including the one intermediate stop at Dousland took just over 30min. All services over the line from Yelverton to Princetown, passenger and freight, were withdrawn on 5 March 1956.

Redlake Tramway

This 7.5-mile long 3ft 0in gauge line was built to link china clay workings on Dartmoor with the GWR at Ivybridge. The line, which rose over its distance from 400ft above sea level to 1,400ft, was opened on 11 September 1911. At the Ivybridge end there was a cable-operated incline but the remainder of the route was locomotive operated. Services continued until closure in 1932.

Right: One of the Churchward-designed 2-6-2T '44xx' class, No 4401, stands in the junction platform at Yelverton with a service from Princetown in August 1953. The small diameter driving wheels of this relatively small class of 11 locomotives limited their use for fast running with the result that they were restricted to hilly branch lines, such as those to Princetown and Looe in the southwest.
Ian Allan Library

Left: Viewed looking towards the buffer stops, GWR 2-6-2T No 4403 is recorded at Princetown station on 15 June 1926.
H. C. Casserley

Redruth & Chasewater Railway

Authorised on 17 June 1824 and opened on 30 January 1826, the nine-mile 4ft 0in gauge Redruth & Chasewater [sic] Railway ran from Redruth to Point Quay, on the River Fal. The line, one of the most important of the early mineral lines in Cornwall, was the first in the county to use wrought-iron edge rails with flanged wheels. Apart from the main line, there were also a number of short branches, including those from Lanner to Wheal Beacham, which opened shortly after the main line, and to Chacewater, which was started in 1853 but abandoned following the failure of the mines that it was designed to serve. An Act of 9 May 1853 permitted steam haulage over the line but the company's financial position deteriorated and, on 19 July 1879, an official receiver was appointed. The line continued to operate under the control of the Official Receiver until 25 September 1915 when the last train operated.

Seaton & Beer Railway

Incorporated on 13 July 1863, the Seaton & Beer Railway was authorised to construct a 4.5-mile long branch from Seaton Junction, on the LSWR main line from Exeter to Salisbury, to Seaton. The line, which was operated from the start by the LSWR, was opened on 16 March 1868. The S&BR was absorbed by the LSWR on 1 January 1888. In 1910 there were nine return workings per weekday with none on Sundays. The single journey time was about 15min. Seaton was a popular holiday destination and to cater for the summer crowds the Southern Railway rebuilt the station in 1937. Freight services over the branch were withdrawn on 3 February 1964 and the line was to close completely with the withdrawal of passenger services on 7 March 1966. Following the lifting of the track, the section from Colyton to Seaton was taken over by the narrow gauge Seaton & District Tramway Co, whose 2ft 9in gauge electric trams were initially introduced at the Seaton end on 20 August 1970 following the operation's transfer from Eastbourne, where it had been previously based.

Sidmouth Railway

Although initially proposed a decade earlier, the 8.25-mile long Sidmouth Railway was incorporated on 29 June 1871 and opened throughout on 6 July 1874. The line, which was steeply graded and operated by the LSWR, saw 11 return workings per day in 1910 to the branch terminus with the average journey between Sidmouth Junction, on the LSWR main line, and Sidmouth taking some 25min. There were two intermediate stations, Ottery St Mary and Tipton St Johns. Although there were proposals for the LSWR to absorb the Sidmouth Railway, the smaller company retained its independence until the Grouping in 1923. Passenger services to Sidmouth were withdrawn on 6 March 1967 and the line was closed completely when the remaining freight services were withdrawn on 8 May 1967.

South Devon Railway

Authorised on 4 July 1844, the South Devon Railway was backed by the Bristol & Exeter Great Western and Bristol & Gloucester Railways. Engineered by Brunel, the line, with its famous sea-wall section at Dawlish, was designed to be operated by atmospheric traction. The line opened from Exeter to Teignmouth on 30 May 1846 (initially with hired locomotives until the atmospheric system was operational from 13 September 1847), thence to Newton Abbot and to Totnes on 20 July 1847. The atmospheric system proved inadequate and locomotive working over the broad gauge line was introduced between Exeter and Teignmouth on 13 September 1847, to Newton Abbot on 10 January 1848 and from there to Plymouth (Laira) on 10 January 1848, when the section from Totnes to Plymouth was also opened. The line was extended through to the SDR's terminus at Millbay on 4 April 1849. A five-mile branch to Torre, authorised in 1846, was opened on 18 December 1848. During its independent existence, the SDR absorbed a number of other railways: the Dartmouth & Torbay (1862); the South Devon & Tavistock (1865); the Launceston & South Devon (1869); and, the Moretonhampstead & South

Right: In order to provide the propulsion required for the atmospheric traction, Brunel constructed a number of engine houses along the route. This is the Starcross engine house, which is now preserved, as recorded in the early 1930s.
Ian Allan Library

Left: The west end of Exeter St David's station on 16 June 1973 sees Class 52 No 1064 *Western Regent* at the head of a service from Paddington to the West of England.
Norman Preedy

Devon (1872). In 1873 a short branch at Totnes was opened serving the quay; this was initially horse operated although locomotives eventually operated over the branch. The Quay line closed in December 1969. On 1 January 1876 the GWR took over the working of the SDR with the company being formally absorbed on 1 August 1878. The main line from Exeter to Plymouth along with the branch to Torre (subsequently extended to Paignton) remain open to passenger services with the majority of trains now operated by the First Great Western franchise.

South Devon & Tavistock Railway

Incorporated on 24 July 1854, the South Devon & Tavistock Railway was empowered to construct a 13-mile line from Plymouth to Tavistock. Constructed to the broad gauge, the line as opened throughout on 22 June 1859. The line had been backed by the South Devon Railway as a means of countering the threat from the LSWR and the line was operated from the outset by the SDR. The line as built included three tunnels and six wooden viaducts; the latter were rebuilt between 1893 and 1910. The SDR absorbed the smaller company on 1 July 1865 and, the following year, powers were obtained to lay a third track to facilitate standard gauge trains when the Devon & Cornwall Railway was completed. The first standard gauge train operated by the LSWR traversed the line on 17 May 1876 and the LSWR continued to use the SD&TR until the completion of the Plymouth, Devonport & South Western Junction Railway. The final elements of the broad gauge were eliminated in 1892. In 1910 there were 12 return workings per weekday between Plymouth and Tavistock, with 13 on Wednesdays and Saturdays and three on Sundays. Of the weekday service five continued to and from Launceston. Passenger services over the line from Tavistock to Plymouth (Tavistock Junction) ceased on 31 December 1962 (although the final timetabled trains, due to operate on the 29th, had to be cancelled as a result of blizzard conditions). The section of

Right: On Saturday 16 August 1975, Class 50 No 50003, at that date still unnamed, passes Dawlish Warren with a down express.
Gavin Morrison

Left: Class 47 No 47484 *Isambard Kingdom Brunel* is recorded passing Dawlish station on 9 September 1978 with the 08.35 service from Penzance to Paddington. The proximity of the line to the beach and sea is all too evident in this view and the low level of the line along with coastal erosion has led to serious problems with flooding and rock fall.
A. Wynn

Right: Teignmouth was the original terminus of the SDR when the first section of line opened on 30 May 1846. This is the view of the station looking in the down direction and shows the station as it was rebuilt in 1884. The line to the right of the up platform accessed the goods shed.
Ian Allan Library

Left: On 30 April 1962 the Manchester-Penzance train enters Plymouth station behind two 'Warship' class diesel-hydraulics. Also visible in the background is No D1000 *Western Enterprise*, then virtually brand-new, and a further 'Warship'. Plymouth North Road station was originally opened on 28 March 1877 and originally constructed in wood. The station was enlarged in 1908 and, in 1938, work started on its reconstruction. However, work was suspended as a result of World War 2 and not resumed until 1956. This view records the reconstruction work, including the tower block, virtually complete. The station lost its 'North Road' suffix in 1958 with the closure of Friary. The track layout has been rationalised significantly since this view was taken.
Brian Haresnape

Below left: The South Devon Railway's main terminus in Plymouth was Millbay, which opened in 1849 and which was also to be served by the Cornwall Railway. Passenger services were to cease using Millbay on 23 April 1941 and freight facilities were withdrawn 25 years later. This view, taken in 1892, records the first standard gauge passenger train to depart from the station during the process of the final conversion of the broad gauge lines to standard gauge.
Ian Allan Library

line from Marsh Mills to Tavistock South closed completely at the same date. The original curve at the Plymouth end, which ran from west to north, was closed on 5 April 1965 when a new east-north curve was opened. The line remains open to serve Tavistock Yard and an ECC site at Marsh Mills; north of Marsh Mills the Plym Valley Railway was first established in 1980 with the intention of reopening section of the line northwards.

Taw Vale Extension Railway

The construction of the line north from the Exeter & Crediton to Barnstaple was amongst the most contentious in the country, with rival companies – and gauges – coming to the fore. In 1846 there were two competing schemes: the broad-gauge North Devon, backed by the GWR, B&ER and SDR, and the standard-gauge Taw Vale Extension, backed by the LSWR. The TVER, pretending to drop the LSWR involvement, gained the backing of the broad-gauge group and secured its Act on 7 August 1846. At this point, the LSWR re-emerged and tried to have both the TVER and Exeter & Crediton lines built to standard gauge. However, on 8 February 1848 the Railway Commissioners ruled that both lines should be broad gauge – causing the cancellation of the planned opening of the standard-gauge section from Crediton to Cowley Bridge Junction that had already been completed – and stalemate ensued. However, the LSWR temporarily lost interest in the further development of its business in North Devon with the result that the E&CR was leased to the B&ER,

Right: The third intermediate station north of Coleford Junction on the line towards Barnstaple was Lapford. Here ex-SECR 'N' class 2-6-0 No 31821, originally built at Ashford Works in October 1922, enters the station at 3.55pm with the 1.10pm freight from Barnstaple to Exeter on 5 June 1964. This must have been one of the last workings for this particular locomotive as it was withdrawn shortly afterwards before being scrapped in October the same year.
J. R. Besley

Right: North of Lapford the next intermediate station was Eggesford. Here 'Battle of Britain' Pacific No 34083 *605 Squadron* is pictured at the head of the 3.25pm freight from Barnstaple to Exeter and Feltham. The train was booked into a siding to permit an up passenger service to pass.
J. R. Besley

converted to broad gauge and formally opened on 12 May 1851. In February 1852 work commenced on the construction of the TVER — now known as the North Devon Railway — and the line opened on 12 July 1854 formally but services did not commence until 1 August 1854. Leased initially by the B&ER and later by Thomas Brassey, the LSWR took over the lease on the line from 1 January 1863 and the track was quickly converted to mixed gauge to permit the first standard gauge train to run to Bideford on 1 March 1863. The line from Crediton to Barnstaple remains open, with passenger services provided by the First Great Western franchise.

Taw Vale Railway & Dock Co

Authorised on 11 June 1838, the TWR&D was empowered to construct a line from Barnstaple to Fremington and an associated dock at Fremington. However, little happened prior to 1845 when, on 21 July, powers were obtained for the construction of a broad gauge line from Barnstaple to Crediton with the intention of selling the line to the GWR-backed proposed North Devon Railway. The line from Fremington to Barnstaple was constructed by the company under its new name — the North Devon Railway & Dock Co — whilst the section from Barnstaple to Crediton passed to the Taw Vale Extension Railway.

Teign Valley Railway

Authorised as a broad gauge line, the Teign Valley Railway was empowered on 13 July 1863 to construct a line from Heathfield to Ashton. The long-drawn out construction process — which required a total of 12 Acts to see it through to completion — resulted in the line finally opening as a standard gauge line on 9 October 1882 with a short freight extension taking it to Teign House, Christow, opening shortly afterwards. Although the LSWR expressed interest in the line, it fell to the GWR to operate the branch as an isolated section until the conversion of the line to Moretonhampstead to standard gauge. The line from Christow to Exeter was opened by the Exeter Railway in 1903. In 1910 there were five return workings per weekday between Christow and Heathfield with a single journey taking 26min over the 7.75-mile long line. Passenger services over the line were withdrawn on 7 August 1958. The section between Trusham and Christow was severed by flood water on 30 September 1960 and closed officially on 1 May 1961. The line closed from Crockham Siding to Trusham on 10 February 1965. The final section — from Heathfield to Crockham Siding — closed completely on 4 December 1967.

Tiverton & North Devon Railway

Originally authorised in the mid-1860s, the T&NDR was re-incorporated on 19 July 1875 to construct a line from Tiverton to the Barnstaple-Taunton line at Morebath Junction. The line opened, as a standard gauge route, on 1 August 1884. The line was operated by the Bristol & Exeter and was formally absorbed by the GWR from 1 July 1894. There was one intermediate station, at Bampton, with most services operating to Dulverton. In 1910 there were six return workings per day between Exeter and Dulverton, with no service on Sundays.

Right: There was originally only one intermediate station between Tiverton and Morebath Junction — Bampton — and on 26 February 1960 0-6-0PT No 7761 was recorded drawing the 1.35pm service from Dulverton to Exeter into the station.
J. Spencer Gilks

The journey time for a single trip between Tiverton and Dulverton over the 10.5-mile long line was around 25min. Passenger services were withdrawn on 7 October 1963 on which date the section between Tiverton and Morebath Junction closed completely.

Torbay & Brixham Railway

Incorporated on 25 July 1864, this two-mile long broad gauge branch from Churston to Brixham was opened on 28 February 1868. The line was very much the work of a local man — R. W. Wolston — who owned the bulk of the shares and who completed the line's construction when the original contractor

Right: One of the Collett-designed 0-4-2Ts, No 1466, stands in the platform at Brixham with a branch service to Churston in August 1953. The station at Brixham was inconveniently located for the town but was to survive until closure of the branch in May 1963.

defaulted. The line was operated by the South Devon Railway from opening until 1876 after which the T&BR operated the line itself until it was sold to the GWR in 1883. In 1910 there were 13 return workings per day with 14 on Wednesdays and Saturdays; there were five return workings per Sunday. The single journey over the branch from Churston took seven minutes. Passenger and freight – predominantly fish – services over the line were withdrawn 13 May 1963.

Treffry's Railways

One of the most influential figures in the development of the china clay industry to the south of Newquay was J. T. Treffry, who was also chairman for a period of the Cornwall Railway. Following the opening of the canal from Par to Ponts Mill on 4 April 1847, a railway from Ponts Mill to Bugle Mollinis (Wheal Virgin) followed on 18 May 1847. The line was extended in 1855 along the canal to Par Harbour. A second line from Newquay Harbour to Hendra Crazy was completed in November 1849. A branch off this line from a junction, originally called Treloggan, opened to East Wheal Rose mine on 26 February 1849. Treffry died in 1850 and, for the next 20 years, his estate, including his railway interests, were administered by the Court of Chancery. It was in the early 1870s that a new entrepreneur, W. R. Roebuck, emerged, forming the Cornwall Minerals Railway to take over and extend the Treffry network.

Tregantle Military Railway

A standard gauge military line was constructed from Wacker, on the Lynher River, to serve two forts – Scraesdon and Tregantle – built to defend the approaches to the harbour at Plymouth. Partly operated by a cable-operated incline and partly by locomotive, the line existed for about a decade from c1893.

West Cornwall Railway

On 3 August 1846 authorisation was given to extend the existing Hayle Railway to the west, to Penzance, and to the east, to Truro. The line, constructed to standard gauge (although the original act stipulated broad gauge, this was subsequently changed provided that the railway was converted to broad gauge should the Cornwall Railway request it), was opened from Redruth to Penzance on 11 March 1852 and eastwards to Truro Road on 25 August 1852 with a final extension to a terminus at Truro Newham opening on 16 April 1855. However, in 1864 when the Cornwall Railway exercised its right to request the line's conversion, the WCR was unable to finance the work. As a result, the GWR, B&ER and SDR obtained powers on 5 July 1865 to take-over the WCR and, on 1 January 1866, the WCR was taken over although it remained a nominally separate company until Nationalisation in 1948. Following considerable reconstruction work, the first broad gauge freight train to Penzance operated on 6 November 1866 with broad gauge passenger services being introduced on 1 March 1867. Thereafter both standard and broad gauge trains operated over the route. The line from Truro to Penzance remains open as the Cornish main line with passenger services today provided by the First Great Western franchise. Also built under the auspices of the West Cornwall Railway was the

Right: Viewed looking in the up direction in 1920, this view of Redruth station shows well the station buildings on both the up and down platforms. The West Cornwall Railway station at Redruth — the second to serve the town — opened on 25 August 1852 with the extension of the line to Truro. Originally the main line was single but was doubled from Redruth west to Carn Brea by 1896 but that east from Redruth to Drump Lane was only doubled in December 1911 (from there to Scorrier, the last section of the main line to be treated with the exception of the Royal Albert Bridge, was doubled in 1913).
Ian Allan Library

St Ives branch. The last branch to be constructed to the broad gauge, the 4.25-mile long line from St Erth opened on 1 June 1877. The line was converted to mixed gauge in October 1888 as far as Lelant Quay and broad gauge was removed during the period 20 to 23 May 1892. In April 1910 there were 13 return workings per day with four on Sundays. A single journey over the steeply graded branch took about 15min. Although freight traffic over the branch ceased in the early 1960s, the line remains open to passenger traffic. The line was slightly foreshortened when, on 23 May 1971, a new station at St Ives was constructed adjacent to the disused goods shed and the original site converted into a car park. A new station, Lelant Saltings, designed to facilitate park-and-ride traffic into St Ives was opened on 13 May 1978. The line is currently operated as part of the First Great Western franchise.

Right: On 16 July 1978, Class 47 No 47510 departs from Penzance with the 15.45 (Sunday) service for Paddington.
Brian Morrison

LOCOMOTIVE SHEDS AND FACILITIES

Appledore
A one-road shed was opened by the Bideford, Westward Ho! & Appledore Railway on 1 May 1908. The shed closed in 1910.

Ashburton
Opened by the Buckfastleigh, Totnes & South Devon Railway on 1 May 1872, this one-road shed, sited to the south of the station, was closed in November 1958. The line from Buckfastleigh to Ashburton was briefly preserved but was to close as a result of road modernisation. The shed, however, still stands.

Ashton
Sited to the south of Ashton station, this one-road shed was opened by the Teign Valley Railway on 9 October 1882. Closed prior to 1910, the building was not demolished until some 50 years later.

Axminster
The LSWR opened a one-road shed east of the station on 19 June 1860. The shed closed in 1896 and, by 1903, when a servicing facility was established in connection with the Lyme Regis branch, was demolished. The servicing facility survived until dieselisation in 1963.

Barnstaple
The town of Barnstaple had three locomotive sheds. The first of these to open – adjacent to Barnstaple Junction station – was opened by the North Devon Railway & Dock Co on 1 August 1854. This was closed in 1863 and replaced by a new two-road shed built adjacent to the original structure. Towards the end of the Southern Railway's existence the shed was reroofed. Barnstaple Junction shed was closed in September 1964 and later demolished. The second site was at the east end of Barnstaple Victoria Road station; this two-road shed was opened by the Devon & Somerset Railway on 1 November 1873. The shed was closed in January 1951 and demolished. The third facility was that serving the narrow-gauge Lynton & Barnstaple. A two-road structure was opened at Pilton Yard on 16 May 1898. Subsequently rebuilt, the shed closed with the line on 30 September 1935. The shed building was to survive until 8 September 1992, when it was destroyed by fire.

Bideford
The first shed in the town was a one-road shed opened by the North Devon Railway & Dock Co on 1 August 1854. The shed was sited to the north of Bideford Cross Parks goods station. The shed was closed c1872 although was to survive as a building until demolition c1960. A second shed in the town was opened by the Bideford, Westward Ho! & Appledore Railway on 20 May 1901. This two-road structure was closed on 27 March 1917 but remains extant in alternative use.

Bodmin

A single-track shed, sited on the west of the line to the south of Bodmin General station, was opened by the GWR on 27 May 1887. The shed was closed in April 1962. After a short period leased by the Great Western Society, the shed was demolished. The site is now owned by the Bodmin & Wenford Railway.

Brixham

A one-road shed, at the south end of the station, was opened by the Torbay & Brixham Railway on 28 February 1868. It was to be demolished in 1896 and replaced by a new structure the following year on the same site. The new shed was in fact the corrugated iron shed that had previously stood at Stenalees. The new facility was to survive until closure on 22 July 1929.

Bude

The LSWR constructed a single-track shed to the south of the station. This was opened on 10 August 1898. The shed closed in September 1964.

Budleigh Salterton

Opened by the Budleigh Salterton Railway on 15 May 1897, a one-road shed was situated at the north end of the station. The shed closed on 1 June 1903 and demolished by the mid-1920s.

Burlescombe

Located at the west end of the station, this one-road shed was opened by the Westleigh Mineral Railway – part of the Bristol & Exeter – in January 1875 to house the 3ft 0in gauge locomotives used in the quarry. It was to survive until October 1898 when the line was rebuilt to standard gauge.

Burngullow

A single-track shed was opened by the Newquay & West Cornwall Railway in July 1869. Sited to the north of the station, the shed passed to the GWR in 1896 and was closed in March 1906. It was demolished in 1929.

Callington

The 3ft 6in gauge East Cornwall Mineral Railway opened a one-road shed on 7 May 1872; this was replaced by a new shed, now located to the east of the station, by the Plymouth, Devonport & South Western Junction Railway, when the line was converted to standard gauge in 1908. The new shed was modified in both 1924 and 1935/36 before being closed by BR in September 1964 and demolished.

Calstock

The 3ft 6in gauge East Cornwall Mineral Railway opened a single-track shed on 7 May 1872. The shed was to close with the line's conversion to standard gauge in 1908.

Carn Brea

Opened in 1838 by the Hayle Railway, a two-road shed was sited to the east of Carn Brea station on the north of the line. It was taken over by the West Cornwall Railway in 1846 and by the GWR 30 years later. Modified in 1896, the shed was to close in August 1917.

Churston

Opened by the Dartmouth & Torbay Railway, a servicing facility existed between 4 March 1861 and 16 August 1864.

Crediton

A one-road shed, situated to the west of the station, was opened by the Exeter, Crediton & Barnstaple Railway on 12 May 1851. Following a fire on 20 August 1862, the shed was rebuilt and reopened in 1874. The shed was to close c1872.

Delabole

Opened by the LSWR on 18 October 1893, this one-road shed was located to the east of Delabole station. The shed was superseded by that at Wadebridge, which opened on 1 June 1895, and was completely closed by 1900.

Exeter

The first temporary shed, a one-road structure, was opened by the Bristol & Exeter Railway adjacent to St David's station on 1 May 1844; this closed in 1851. It was replaced by a new three-road shed, to the west of the station. This was itself closed and demolished in 1864 and replaced by a new four-road shed further to the north. This new shed was extended in 1894 and was to survive until closure on 14 October 1963. Subsequently demolished, a small diesel maintenance depot was later built on the site. To the south of the station, on the east side of the line, the South Devon Railway opened a one-road shed in July 1846; this was also to close in 1864. On 19 July 1860, the Exeter & Yeovil Railway opened a three-road shed to the east of Queen Street station. This shed was to close in 1887 with the opening of the shed at Exmouth Junction and with a servicing point, with turntable, established at Queen Street station. The 1860 shed was demolished in 1900 although the servicing point continued in use for a further three decades.

Exmouth

The Exeter & Exmouth Railway opened a one-road shed on the east side of the station on 1 July 1861. This was to survive until it was rebuilt in 1927. Following reroofing at about the time of Nationalisation, the shed was closed on 8 November 1963 and demolished.

Exmouth Junction

Opened on 3 November 1887, this large, 11-road shed was constructed by the LSWR. Built out of corrugated iron, the building had deteriorated by the 1920s and was to be closed in 1927 following the construction of a new 12-road shed slightly to the east. The new shed was to survive as a steam shed until June 1965 and was to be closed completely in March 1967. It was later demolished.

Falmouth

The shed, situated at the west end of the station on the south of the line, was first opened by the Cornwall Railway on 24 August 1863. The two-road shed was modified in 1897 when a larger turntable was added. The shed closed on 21 September 1925 but was to continue as a servicing point until demolition in 1932. A water tower and engine pit survived after the shed was demolished, not finally closing until after Nationalisation.

Fowey

A one-road shed, sited to the east of the station, was opened by the Cornwall Minerals Railway prior to 1874. Its closure date is unknown but it was demolished just prior to World War 1.

Goodrington Sands

A servicing area, with turntable, existed on the west side of the line, to the south of Goodrington Sands halt between 1957 and c1964.

Hayle

The West Cornwall Railway had opened a one-road shed by 1879; it survived in use until 1896 and was officially closed in 1906.

Helston

A one-road shed was opened by the Helston Railway on 9 May 1887. The shed, on the west of the line to the north of the station, closed in December 1963.

Hemyock

A one-road shed, situated at the west end of the station, was opened by the Culm Valley Light Railway on 29 May 1876. The shed closed on 21 October 1929.

Holsworthy

Opened by the LSWR on 20 January 1879, this one-road shed was sited to the east of the station. Although probably closed officially in 1898 with the opening of the shed in Bude, the turntable was not removed until 1915 and the shed itself ceased to function in 1917 when it was converted into a store. The building was demolished c1923.

Ilfracombe

A one-road shed, sited adjacent to the station, was opened by the Barnstaple & Ilfracombe Railway on 24 July 1874. It was demolished in 1928 and replaced by a new one-road shed located to the south of the station. This was to be closed in 1964.

Kingsbridge

A one-road shed, sited on the south side of the station, was opened on 19 December 1893. The shed was to survive until closure in September 1961. It was later demolished.

Kingswear

Opened by the Dartmouth & Torbay Railway on 16 August 1864, this one-road shed was closed on 14 July 1924 and demolished seven years later.

Launceston

There were two sheds serving the town. The earlier of the two, first opened on 1 June 1865 by the Launceston & South Devon Railway, was a single-track shed situated to the east of the L&SDR station. This was extended by the GWR in 1899. The shed was officially closed on 13 December 1962 but it continued in use until September 1964. The LSWR shed, sited to the east of the LSWR station, was opened on 21 July 1886. The single-track shed, later modified with the addition of a turntable and coal stage, was to survive until the 1950s and the turntable continued in use until 1963.

Liskeard

A one-road shed was opened by the Cornwall Railway on the south side of the line to the east of the station in May 1859. Its small turntable was removed in 1909 and the shed ceased to have a locomotive allocation from 10 October 1912, although it was not officially closed until 1918.

Looe

Situated to the south of Looe station and opened by the Liskeard & Looe Railway in November 1901, this one-road shed was closed shortly prior to its demolition in late 1919.

Lynton

The narrow-gauge Lynton & Barnstaple Railway opened a one-road shed at Lynton on 16 May 1898. Following track remodelling in 1904, the shed was to survive until the line's closure on 30 September 1935.

Meldon Quarry

Opened in March 1927 by the Southern Railway, a one-road shed was constructed to house the departmental shunter that worked the quarry. The shed was rebuilt shortly after Nationalisation and, after the end of steam in 1966, the shed continued in use, housing a diesel shunter.

Moorswater

A two-road shed was opened by the Liskeard & Caradon Railway on 27 December 1860 but this was to be replaced in March 1862 by a second shed located to the east of the original structure, which became the locomotive and wagon works of the Liskeard & Looe Railway. The second shed was to close on 11 September 1961.

Moretonhampstead

A one-road shed, sited to the east of the station, was opened by the Moretonhampstead & South Devon Railway on 4 July 1866. The shed, which was closed in November 1947, has been used subsequently as a garage.

Newquay

The Cornwall Minerals Railway opened a one-road shed on the west of the line at the south end of the station on 1 June 1874. This shed closed in 1904 and was demolished. The following year, the GWR opened a new two-road shed further south. This was officially closed on 22 September 1930 and was demolished in August 1936.

Newton Abbot

A small two-road shed was opened by the South Devon Railway to the north of the station on 30 December 1846. This was replaced in November 1893 by a new six-road shed located further west. The new shed was to survive until closure on 1 April 1962 with a new diesel depot constructed alongside. This itself closed in the 1980s and, following closure, the site of both the steam shed and diesel depot was cleared in the late 1990s.

Okehampton

A servicing point was initially established in the late 1870s to the east of the station before the opening of a one-road shed slightly further to the east in 1894. The new shed was enlarged in 1914 before being destroyed by fire in 1920. The shed was rebuilt in 1920 and modified in 1943. It was finally to close in 1964.

Padstow

A servicing area, with turntable, was established by the LSWR to the east of the station in 1900. The turntable was relocated further south in 1933 and enlarged, after World War 2, to accommodate the Bulleid Pacifics. The turntable ceased to be used in the early 1960s.

Penzance

The West Cornwall Railway opened its first shed, a single-road building, to the east of the station in March 1852. This was supplemented by the a new two-road shed located to the north of the line to the east of the station in 1866. The original shed was to close in 1876 when the second shed was itself replaced by a new two-road shed. The constrained nature of the site precluded any further development and, in June 1914, a new four-road shed was opened at Long Rock, about 1.25 miles from Penzance station. This shed was to close to steam on 10 September 1962 but was to survive, until demolition in 1976, as a diesel depot.

Plymouth

Although there was probably a temporary facility at Laira Green with the opening of the South Devon Railway on 5 May 1848, this would have lasted only until the opening of the extension to Millbay the following year. A two-road shed was established at Millbay, to the north of the station by the SDR. The GWR opened a second shed at the site, adjacent to the existing SDR structure. The latter was rebuilt towards the end of the 19th century. The facility at Millbay was officially closed in 1924 but remained in use until 1931 when Laira was extended. The first shed, a roundhouse, at Laira opened in 1901. It was extended in 1931 with the addition of a four-road shed. The steam shed was closed in April 1964 and replaced by a new diesel depot with the original buildings retained for stabling purposes. A one-road shed was opened by the SDR at Plymouth Dock in 1869; this was slightly extended in the early 20th century. Closed in 1955, the building was taken over as a workshop by the port authority. Adjacent to Devonport station, the LSWR opened a two-road shed on 17 May 1876; this was to survive as the main LSWR shed in the city until the opening of the shed at Friary in 1891 but was not to close finally until 1908. The first Friary shed, a two-road structure located to the south of the station, opened on 1 July 1891. This shed was to close when a new shed, located further to the east, was opened in 1908. The new shed, with three roads, was reroofed shortly after Nationalisation before being closed on 6 May 1963. It was later demolished.

Princetown

The Princetown Railway opened a one-road shed to the south of the station on 11 August 1883. The shed was closed on 11 March 1956 and subsequently demolished.

Seaton

The Seaton & Beer Railway opened a one-road shed to the east of the station on 16 March 1868. This was to survive until 1937 when it was demolished and replaced by a new one-road shed sited slightly to the north. This was closed on 14 November 1963 and subsequently demolished.

Sidmouth

A one-road shed was opened by the LSWR on 6 July 1874. This was destroyed by fire on 7 January 1900 and replaced by a new one-road structure. Use of the shed and its facilities ceased by the mid-1930s with the building let out for commercial use. It is still standing.

St Blazey

A nine-track semi-roundhouse was opened by the Cornwall Minerals Railway on 1 June 1874. The facility was supplemented by the addition of a three-road shed sited to the north of the original structure, which functioned between c1877 and c1896, after which date it was used as workshops. The original roundhouse was closed to steam in April 1962 and was used thereafter, until complete closure on 25 April 1987, as a diesel depot. Following closure of the roundhouse, diesel maintenance facilities were transferred to the later three-road shed and the original roundhouse, now listed, was converted for new industrial use. The turntable remains operational.

St Dennis Junction

A servicing facility, with water tower and coal stage, existed here although no dates are known.

St Ives

The GWR opened a one-track shed to the south of the station on 1 June 1877. The shed was to close in September 1961 and was subsequently demolished.

Stenalees

A single-track shed was opened by the Newquay & Cornwall Junction Railway just south of Goonbarrow Junction, on the Gunheath branch, in October 1869. The shed was closed in October 1896 when the corrugated iron structure was relocated to Brixham.

Stoke Canon

Sited slightly to the north of Stoke Canon station, this one-road shed was opened by the Bristol & Exeter Railway in 1860. Closed in 1879, the building was used as a goods shed after 1894.

Tavistock

A one-road shed was opened by the South Devon & Tavistock Railway on 22 June 1859. Sited to the south of the station, the shed was closed in July 1865 and demolished c1900.

Teignmouth

Located in the vicinity of the station, a locomotive servicing facility for the South Devon Railway existed here between 30 May 1846 and 19 March 1847.

Tiverton Junction

Situated at the south end of Tiverton Junction station, a one-road shed was opened by the Bristol & Exeter Railway on 12 June 1848. This shed, which lost its turntable in May 1908, was closed in 1932 and replaced by a new one-road shed sited slightly to the west. This shed was to survive until closure in October 1964.

Torre

The South Devon Railway opened a servicing facility with turntable at the south end of Torre station in 1848. The facility closed in 1864 but the turntable remained in use probably until removal in 1883.

Torrington

Opened by the LSWR on 18 July 1872, a one-road shed was situated to the west of Torrington station. Originally provided with a turntable, this was removed in 1925. The shed was closed on 2 November 1959.

Totnes

A two-road shed, sited to the south of the station, was opened by the South Devon Railway on 20 July 1847. The shed was closed in 1904 and later demolished.

Truro

The first two-road shed on the main line was opened by the Cornwall Railway on the north side of Truro station on 4 May 1859. It was replaced by a new three-road shed, sited to the west of the station in May 1900 and subsequently demolished. The replacement shed, which also included wagon repair facilities, was to survive until closure in November 1965. It was subsequently demolished. A separate facility also existed on the Newham branch; a single-road shed was opened by the West Cornwall Railway on 16 April 1855. Located to the south of Newham station, the shed at Newham closed at some date after the opening of the Cornwall Railway. There was also a facility at Penwithers Junction, to the west of Truro, but little is known of this.

Wadebridge

The Bodmin & Wadebridge Railway opened its first shed on 4 July 1834; this one-road shed was to survive until replacement on 1 June 1895 but was not to be demolished until 1962. The new shed, with two roads, was sited further to the south and on the east side of the station. The shed was further modified in 1906 to accommodate steam railcars, which survived until 1919, and was refurbished in 1949. The shed was closed in October 1964 and later demolished.

Left: Recorded on 12 August 1963, a year before the shed's closure, the single-road shed at Bude plays host to 'N' class 2-6-0 No 31835.
P. Paye

THE BEECHING REPORT

Published in 1963, the Beeching report The Reshaping of British Railways recommended that the following lines within Devon and Cornwall should have all passenger services removed:

- Taunton-Barnstaple Junction
- Liskeard-Looe
- Lostwithiel-Fowey
- St Erth-St Ives
- Okehampton-Plymouth
- Barnstaple Junction-Ilfracombe
- Okehampton-Padstow
- Okehampton-Bude
- Barnstaple Junction-Torrington

- Axminster-Lyme Regis
- Seaton Junction-Seaton (Devon)
- Sidmouth Junction-Sidmouth
- Tipton St John's-Exmouth
- Exeter Central-Exmouth
- Bere Alston-Callington
- Halwill-Torrington
- Bodmin Road/Bodmin North-Wadebridge-Padstow

The following lines were already under threat of closure or closed at the time of the report's completion:

- Tiverton Junction-Hemyock
- Exeter St Davids-Dulverton
- Churston-Brixham
- Brent-Kingsbridge

- Launceston-Plymouth (GWR) (already closed)
- Truro-Chacewater-Newquay (Cornwall) (already closed)
- Helston-Gwinear Road (already closed)

The following passenger services were to be modified:

- Salisbury-Exeter Central
- Exeter Central-Okehampton
- Exeter Central-Barnstaple Junction
- Taunton-Exeter St Davids

- Exeter St Davids-Kingswear
- Plymouth-Penzance
- Par-Newquay (Cornwall)

Of the lines slated for closure, all were to succumb between the publication of the report and the closure of the Ilfracombe line in 1970 with the exception of the lines between St Erth and St Ives, Liskeard and Looe and Exeter Central and Exmouth. Also reprieved was the section of line between Bere Alston and Gunnislake on the line to Callington. However, the section of line to Okehampton was to lose its passenger services entirely albeit remaining open for freight traffic.

PRESERVATION

The counties of Devon and Cornwall possess a considerable variety of preservation schemes with no fewer than five standard gauge schemes as well as three narrow gauge lines rebuilt on erstwhile standard gauge track and a partial reconstruction of the much-mourned Lynton & Barnstaple.

Of the standard gauge lines, the first to be opened was the Dart Valley Railway. Following closure of the branch from Totnes to Ashburton to freight traffic on 10 September 1962, the track was left intact and, following protracted negotiations, the line was acquired by the Dart Valley Railway. Passenger services over the line to Buckfastleigh from a new station at Totnes – now known as Totnes (Littlehempston) – commenced on 5 April 1969. However, plans to run through to the original terminus at Ashburton were thwarted by Devon County Council. A decade earlier the council had opposed closure of the line but now saw the trackbed as a means of improving the A38 road and, following a public enquiry, permission to reuse the erstwhile railway for this purpose was granted. On 2 October 1971 special trains ran to mark the final closure of the section of line from Buckfastleigh to Ashburton. Except for a brief period in the mid-1980s when services operated to and from the original station in Totnes, the line has continued to operate over the section from the new 1969 station through to Buckfastleigh. Today the line is operated by the South Devon Railway, the original Dart Valley Railway Company having taken on the much more ambitious scheme to operate the line between Paignton and Kingswear with its associated bus and ferry services.

As elsewhere, traffic on the Paignton-Kingswear section had been in decline for some years and, despite endeavours to reduce costs, by 1971 the service had declined to a shuttle between Paignton and the branch terminus. During 1971 BR decided to obtain permission to close the line but the DVR stepped in with an offer to purchase and operate the line. In January 1972 the Secretary of State for Transport gave authorisation for the line's closure but services continued, with a Devon County Council subsidy, pending transfer to the DVR. On 28 October 1972 BR relinquished control of the line but continued to operate it from 30 October temporarily whilst the DVR undertook work to facilitate independent operation. The DVR formally began operating its own trains on 1 January 1973. Since then the line, now known as the Paignton & Dartmouth Railway, has become one of the most successful tourist attractions in the region.

Following the withdrawal of the last china clay traffic from Wenford Bridge to Bodmin Road in 1983, a preservation society was launched in June 1984 with the intention of preserving the line. The first limited services were operated within the confines of Bodmin General station in 1987. On 1 September 1989, following the granting of the line's first Light Railway Order, services began to operate over a section of the line from Bodmin General towards Bodmin Road. Since then the line has expanded to include operation from Bodmin Road through to Boscarne Junction. The railway has had ambitious plans for further development – including examination of reopening of the lines to Wenford Bridge and Wadebridge – although these proposals are complicated by the reuse of the disused trackbeds as long-distance footpaths and cycleways.

The smallest of the current standard-gauge projects in Devon and Cornwall is the Plym Valley Railway, which is sited at Marsh Mills. The railway is currently planning on restoring the 1.5-mile long section from Marsh Mills to Plym Bridge with services currently operating over a short section north from Marsh Mills.

The most recent addition to the number of standard gauge preservation schemes in Devon is the Dartmoor Railway. Following the closure of the line through Meldon to passenger services, the line was retained to a quarry for the shipment of ballast. Okehampton, the most important intermediate station on the section between Coleford Junction and Meldon, also survived and was used periodically for the running of summer only services to and from Exeter. In the summer First Great Western still operates a service to and from Okehampton and limited freight traffic to and from Meldon also continues. The Dartmoor Railway has running powers for the section from Coleford Junction to Meldon and is based at Okehampton, however at the time of writing its future is uncertain as a result of its owners — Ealing Community Transport — deciding to terminate services

Apart from the standard gauge preservation schemes in Devon and Cornwall, there are also three schemes that have resurrected short sections of closed standard gauge lines and reopened them as narrow gauge lines. The most easterly of these is the Seaton Tramway. The Seaton Tramway had its origins in a two-foot gauge tramway originally operated at Eastbourne by the late Claude Lane. He had had experience of operating 15in gauge trams at garden fetes and other events and was looking for a permanent base. The first section at Eastbourne opened in 1954 and further extensions followed. However, tenure on the Eastbourne site was running out and, in the mid-1960s, an alternative location was sought. Negotiations to acquire part of the branch from Seaton proved successful and, on 24 December 1969, the Seaton & District Electric Tramway Co was borne. The new tramway — now built to a gauge of 2ft 9in — first operated with battery power on 9 April 1971 and overhead operation from Seaton Riverside to Colyford commenced on 23 September 1973. The line was extended to its town centre terminus on 17 May 1975 and, finally, to Colyton in 1980.

Constructed on part of the trackbed of the Newquay-Chacewater line, the 15in gauge Lappa Valley Steam Railway runs from a station at Benny Halt to East Wheal Rose, a distance of about one mile. The line has been operational since 1974. More recently, the Launceston Steam Railway has been established on part of the closed ex-LSWR line to the west of Launceston. This 1ft 11.5in gauge line opened from its station in Launceston, sited to the west of the original station on the site of the gasworks siding, initially on 26 December 1983. This 0.75-mile route was extended to the Newchurches loop, a further 0.75 mile, on 2 July 1986 and to its final terminus, New Mills, in June 1995. The line now runs for a total of three miles.

Had the original Lynton & Barnstaple survived World War 2 then, undoubtedly, it would have become a candidate for immediate preservation on closure. The fact, however, that it closed in 1935 and was quickly dismantled meant that little, other than the trackbed and some of the line's infrastructure, survived. Interest in the line remained strong and, in 1979, the L&BR Association was formed. Woody Bay station was acquired in 1995 and, following restoration, services from the station were launched in 2004. The line was extended to a total of a mile in 2006 to a temporary terminus at Killington Lane, to the west of Woody Bay. The company has ambitious plans for the ultimate reopening of about nine miles of line from a new terminus in Lynton closer to the town and Blackmoor Gate.

MAPS

LEGEND

▬▬▬	Closed line
▬▬▬	Passenger line
▬▬▬	Preserved line
▬▬▬	Freight line
New Quay ●	Station open
(1923)	Date station opened
Holsworthy ○	Station closed
[1964]	Date station closed
1857	Date railway line opened
Clo 1989	Date railway line closed
A30	Main road / road number
M5	Motorway /motorway junction / motorway number
×▬▬▬ⅹ	Level crossing / bridge
〜〜〜	Water Trough

■	Locomotive shed
GREAT WESTERN	Railway company name
Abbreviations used on maps	
c.	circa (around)
Clly	Colliery
G	Goods
HL	High Level (station)
LL	Low Level (station)
J	Junction - used with signalbox name
Junc	Junction - as used in station name
Sdg	Siding
Std G.	Standard gauge
Tnl	Tunnel
UL	Uncertain location

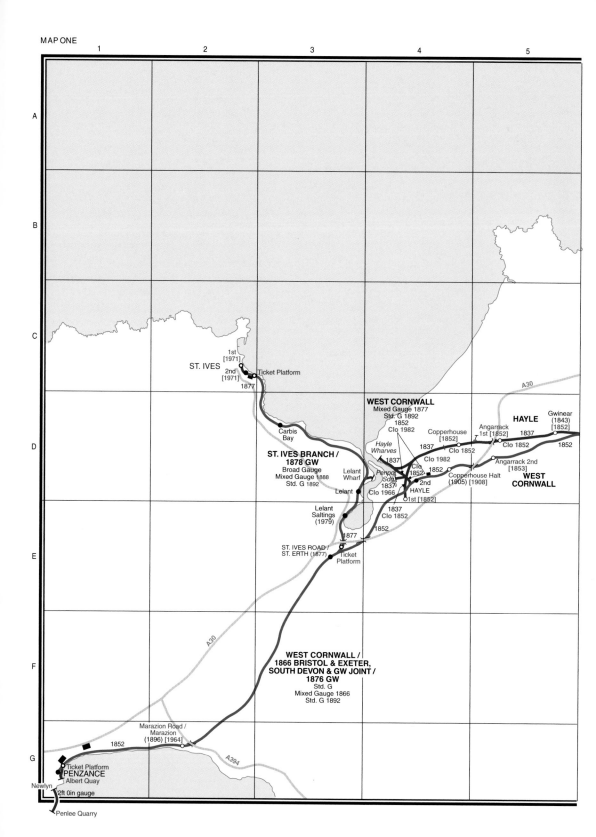

1   2   3   4   5

A

B

C

ST. IVES
1st [1971]
2nd [1971]   Ticket Platform
1877

Carbis Bay

WEST CORNWALL
Mixed Gauge 1877
Std. G 1892
1852
Clo 1982

HAYLE   Gwinear (1843) [1852]

Copperhouse [1852]   Angarrack 1st [1852]   1837
1837   Clo 1852   Clo 1852   1852

ST. IVES BRANCH / 1878 GW
Broad Gauge
Mixed Gauge 1888
Std. G 1892

Hayle Wharves
1837

Clo 1982   Angarrack 2nd [1853]

Lelant Wharf   *Penpol Sdg*
Clo 1852   1852   **WEST CORNWALL**
1837   Copperhouse Halt
Lelant   Clo 1966   2nd   (1905) [1908]
1st [1852]   **HAYLE**
1837
Lelant Saltings (1979)   Clo 1852
1852
1877
ST. IVES ROAD / ST. ERTH (1877)   Ticket Platform

A30

D

E

WEST CORNWALL / 1866 BRISTOL & EXETER, SOUTH DEVON & GW JOINT / 1876 GW
Std. G
Mixed Gauge 1866
Std. G 1892

A30

F

Marazion Road / Marazion (1896) [1964]
1852

A394

G
Ticket Platform
PENZANCE
Albert Quay
Newlyn
2ft 0in gauge

Penlee Quarry

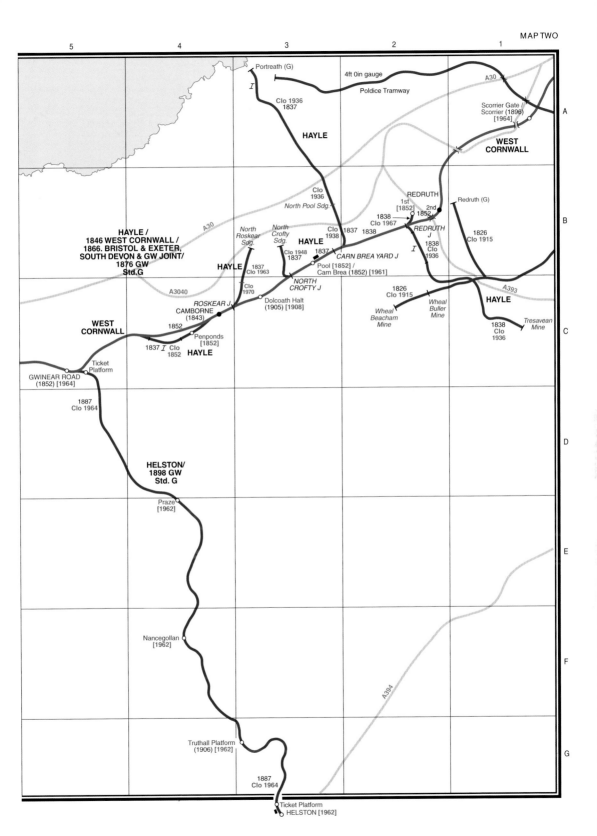

5 4 3 2 1

Portreath (G)

4ft 0in gauge

A30

Scorrier Gate /
Scorrier (1896)
[1964]

Clo 1936
1837

Poldice Tramway

HAYLE

**WEST
CORNWALL**

A

Clo
1936

North Pool Sdg.

REDRUTH
1st
[1852]   2nd
1852

Redruth (G)

A30

1838
Clo 1967

1826
Clo 1915

B

**HAYLE /
1846 WEST CORNWALL /
1866. BRISTOL & EXETER,
SOUTH DEVON & GW JOINT/
1876 GW
Std.G**

North
Roskear
Sdg.

North
Crofty
Sdg.

Clo
1938

HAYLE

1837 1838

1838

*REDRUTH
J*

1838
Clo
1936

HAYLE

1837
Clo 1963

Clo 1948
1837

1837

CARN BREA YARD J

Pool [1852] /
Carn Brea (1852) [1961]

A3040

A30

Clo
1970

Dolcoath Halt
(1905) [1908]

*NORTH
CROFTY J*

1826
Clo 1915

*Wheal
Beacham
Mine*

*Wheal
Buller
Mine*

HAYLE

ROSKEAR J
CAMBORNE
(1843)

A393

C

**WEST
CORNWALL**

1852

Penponds
[1852]

1838
Clo
1936

*Tresavean
Mine*

1837 Clo
1852

HAYLE

Ticket
Platform

GWINEAR ROAD
(1852) [1964]

1887
Clo 1964

D

**HELSTON/
1898 GW
Std. G**

Praze
[1962]

E

F

Nancegollan
[1962]

A394

Truthall Platform
(1906) [1962]

G

1887
Clo 1964

Ticket Platform
HELSTON [1962]

1   2   3   4   5

Clo1919
WEST J
BLACKWATER
CHACEWATER
[1964]

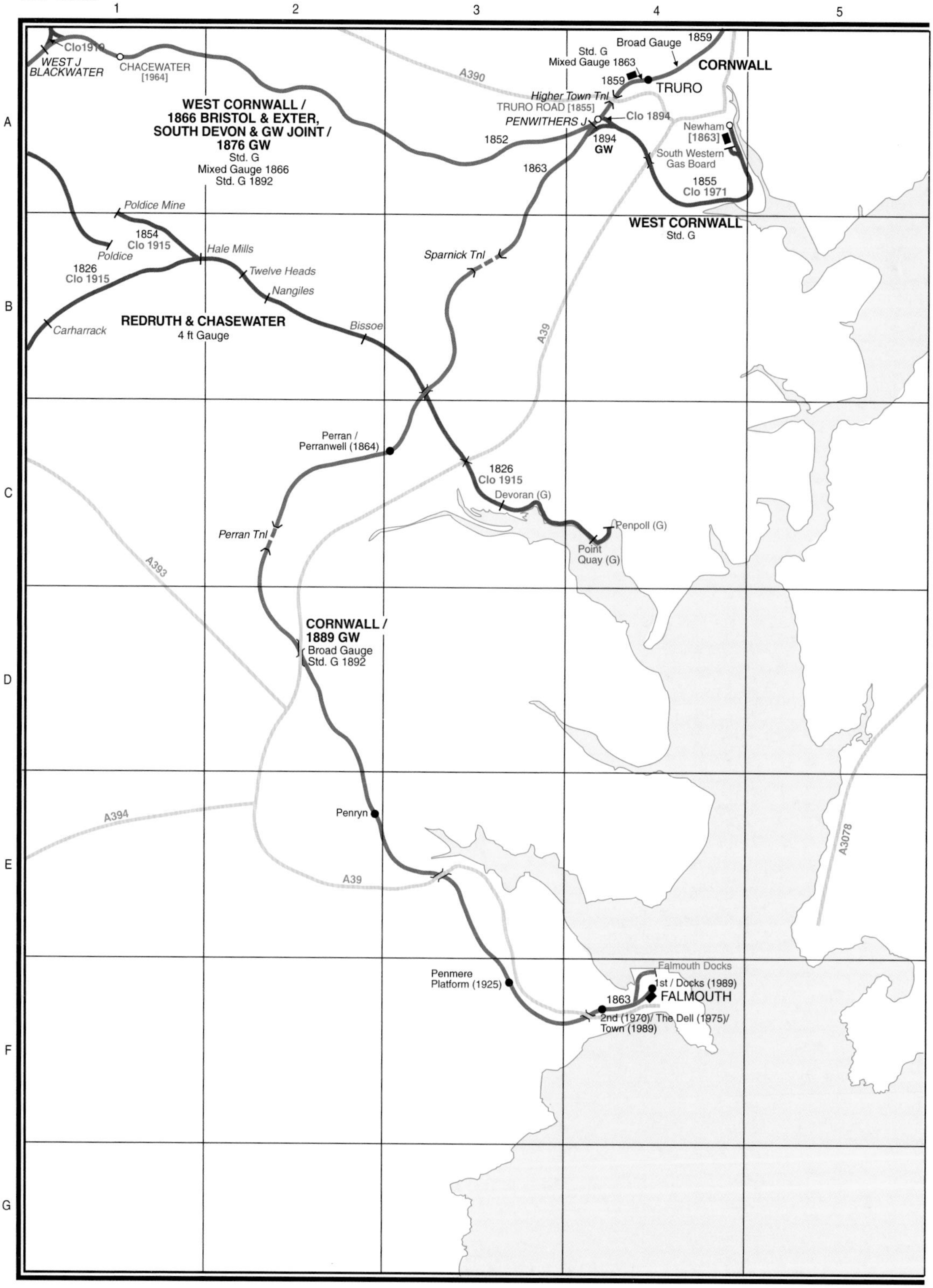

Broad Gauge
1859

Std. G
Mixed Gauge 1863
1859

CORNWALL

**WEST CORNWALL /
1866 BRISTOL & EXTER,
SOUTH DEVON & GW JOINT /
1876 GW**
Std. G
Mixed Gauge 1866
Std. G 1892

A390

Higher Town Tnl
TRURO ROAD [1855]
PENWITHERS J.

TRURO

Clo 1894

Newham
[1863]

1852

1894
GW

South Western
Gas Board

Poldice Mine

1863

1855
Clo 1971

1854
Clo 1915
Poldice

Hale Mills

Sparnick Tnl

WEST CORNWALL
Std. G

1826
Clo 1915

Twelve Heads

Nangiles

A39

REDRUTH & CHASEWATER
4 ft Gauge

Bissoe

Carharrack

Perran /
Perranwell (1864)

1826
Clo 1915
Devoran (G)

Penpoll (G)

Perran Tnl

Point
Quay (G)

A393

**CORNWALL /
1889 GW**
Broad Gauge
Std. G 1892

A394

Penryn

A39

A3078

Penmere
Platform (1925)

Falmouth Docks
1st / Docks (1989)
FALMOUTH

1863

2nd (1970)/ The Dell (1975)/
Town (1989)

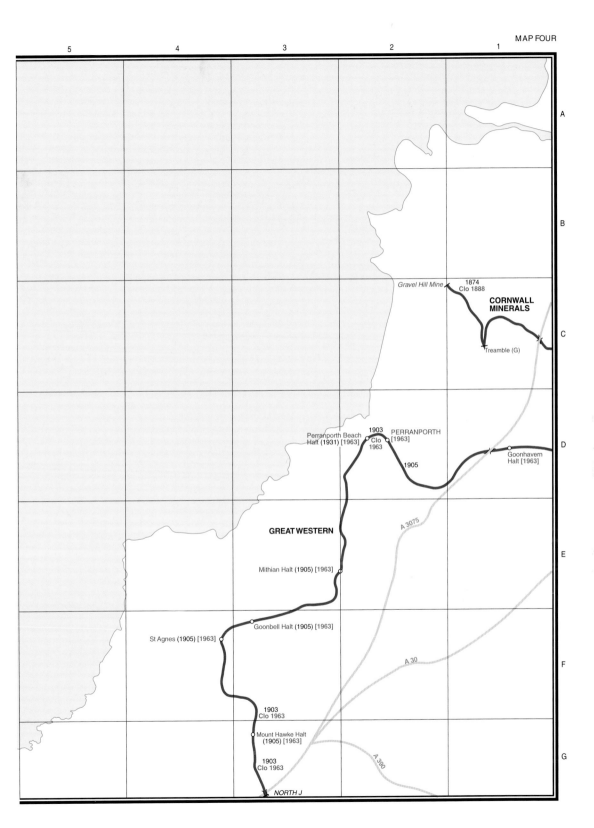

5   4   3   2   1

A

B

Gravel Hill Mine   1874
Clo 1888

**CORNWALL
MINERALS**

C

Treamble (G)

Perranporth Beach   1903   **PERRANPORTH**
Halt (1931) [1963]   Clo   [1963]
     1963

Goonhavern
Halt [1963]

D

1905

A 3075

GREAT WESTERN

E

Mithian Halt (1905) [1963]

Goonbell Halt (1905) [1963]

St Agnes (1905) [1963]

A 30

F

1903
Clo 1963

Mount Hawke Halt
(1905) [1963]

1903
Clo 1963

A 390

G

NORTH J

1 2 3 4 5

Harbour

1849
Clo 1926
Newquay Tnl

A 3059

A 3059

A 39

NEWQUAY
(1876)

A

1849

A 3058

A 392

TOLCARN J
1857 Clo 1963
NEWQUAY J
LANE J
1874 Clo 1963
CM
1905
*Trevemper
Deviation*

1849

Quintrel Downs
Platform (1911)

CM

1874

Trevemper Siding

1849
Clo 1905
GW

A 392

A 392

1849
Clo 1874
Toldish Tnl

A 3075

**TREFFRY'S /
1873 CORNWALL
MINERALS /
1896 GW**

Halloon (1876) /
St Columb Road
(1878)

St Columb
Brick Works

B

TREFFRY'S

Trewerry & Trerice
Halt (1905) [1963]

Benny Halt

A 3058

A 30

Clo 1982

Retew

**GREAT
WESTERN**

1874

Lappa Valley
Railway

1849
Clo 1963

A 3076

Melangoose Mill

C

**CORNWALL
MINERALS**

1874
Clo 1952

1874
Clo 1963

Clo
1905
1849

Mitchell &
Newlyn Halt
(1905) [1963]
*East Wheal
Rose Mine*

SHEPHERDS (1905) [1963]

D

1905 Clo 1963

A 30

A 3058

A 39

E

Grampound
Road
[1964]

CORNWALL
Broad Gauge
Std. G 1892

A 390

F

Probus & Ladock
Platform (1908) [1957]

Polperro Tnl

G

1859
Buckshead Tnl

A 390

A 3078

Four

5   4   3   2   1

Victoria (1876) /
Roche (1904)

**CORNWALL MINERALS /
1896 GW**

A30

A391

A

**CORNWALL
MINERALS**

1849 BODMIN ROAD J /
ST DENNIS J

Carbis Wharf

1874

BUGLE (1876)
Mollinis

**TREFFRY'S /
1873 CORNWALL
MINERALS /
1896 GW**

1874
Pochins
Siding

1874
Old Beam Siding

1842 **TREFFRY'S**

*Luxulyan
Quarry*

B

3ft 0in
gauge

1893

GOONBARROW J

1842

Clo 1982

*Higher Gothers
Clay Works*

Clo 1973

1842

Bridges (1876) /
Luxulyan (1905)

TREFFRY'S

1849
Clo 1965

**CORNWALL
MINERALS**

*New Caudledown
South Sdg.*
Clo 1965

Luxulyan Tnl (1946)
(Opened out 1958)

1874

Parkandillack

Stenalees

**CORNWALL
MINERALS**

1842
Clo 1874

*Hendra
Down*

C

1874

1912

**CORNWALL
MINERALS**

Gunheath Sdg.

1893

Goonbarrow Tnl

1893
Clo 1965

Carbean Sdg.

Seven

Drinnick Wharf

1869

**GREAT
WESTERN**

1874

Lansalson (G)

**NEWQUAY & CORNWALL JUNCTION /
1874 CORNWALL MINERALS /
1896 GW**

Clo
1964

1920

Carloggas

1869

Broad Gauge
Std. G 1892

Boskell Sdg.

1912
Clo c. 1982

1920
Clo 1968

Bojea Sdg.

*Meledor
Mill*

1921

**GREAT
WESTERN**

A391

A390

D

*New Meledor
Sdg*

1869

CORNWALL

TRENANCE J

A3082

A3058

1st (1863) [1901]
2nd (1901) [1931]
BURNGULLOW

ST AUSTELL

(G) [1968]

1859

CORNWALL

A390

**CORNWALL /
1889 GW**
Broad Gauge
Std. G 1892

A390

E

*Pentewan
Tramway*

F

A390

Pentewan

G

1   2   3   4   5

A 30

**BODMIN & WADEBRIDGE /
1886 LONDON & SOUTH WESTERN /
1923 SR**

A

1834
Clo 1967   [LSW] / North added
(1949) [1967]

A 389

BODMIN

[GW] / General
added (1949) [1967]   **GREAT WESTERN**
**To Private
(Bodmin & Wenford
Railway)**

Ticket
Platform

1888   1887
Clo 1983   Clo 1983

Colesloggett
Halt

B

A 38   A 38

**CORNWALL /
1889 GW**
Broad Gauge
Std. G 1892

A 30

1887
Clo 1983

1859

BODMIN ROAD (1859) /
BODMIN PARKWAY (1983)

Respryn [1859]

A 390

Brownqueen Tnl

C

Six

D

LOSTWITHIEL

1859

**LOSTWITHIEL & FOWEY /
1893 CORNWALL MINERALS /
1896 GW**
Broad Gauge
Std. G 1895

*Colcerrow
Quarry*

E

TREFFRY'S
Carmears

Treverrin Tnl

Clo 1874

Ponts Mill

1869

1874

PONTS MILL J

F

TREFFRY'S

A 390

1842

Golant (1896) /
Halt added (1955)
[1965]

ST. BLAZEY
(1876)[1925]   **CM**
1879   PAR

**CORNWALL
MINERALS**

BRIDGE J

1869

1874
Clo 1968   *Pinnock Tnl*

*Carne
Point*

1842

G

CORNWALL

*Par
Harbour*

A 3082

1895
Clo 1968   **GREAT WESTERN**

1874   FOWEY (1876) [1965]

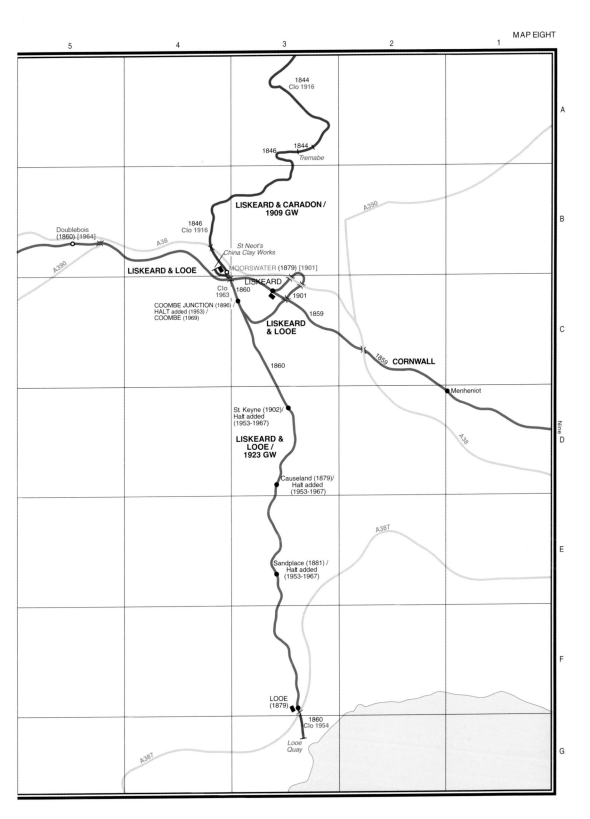

5   4   3   2   1

A

1844
Clo 1916

1846   1844
Tremabe

**LISKEARD & CARADON /
1909 GW**

A390

B

Doublebois
(1860) [1964]

1846
Clo 1916

A38

A390

*St Neot's
China Clay Works*

LISKEARD & LOOE

MOORSWATER (1879) [1901]

LISKEARD

Clo
1963 1860   1901

COOMBE JUNCTION (1896) /
HALT added (1953) /
COOMBE (1969)

1859

**LISKEARD
& LOOE**

C

1859 **CORNWALL**

1860

Menheniot

Nine

St. Keyne (1902)/
Halt added
(1953-1967)

**LISKEARD &
LOOE /
1923 GW**

D

A38

Causeland (1879)/
Halt added
(1953-1967)

A387

E

Sandplace (1881) /
Halt added
(1953-1967)

F

LOOE
(1879)

1860
Clo 1954

*Looe
Quay*

A387

G

1 2 3 4 5

EAST CORNWALL MINERAL/
1894 PLYMOUTH, DEVONPORT
& SOUTH WESTERN JUNCTION/
1923 SR
3 ft 6 inch Gauge
Std.G 1908

1872
Clo 1908

*Morwellham
Quay*

1908

Quay Calstock

A390

PLYMOUTH, DEVONPORT &
SOUTH WESTERN JUNCTION/
1923 SR

1908

BEER ALSTON/
BERE ALSTON (1897)

1908

A388

Eight

A38

Ernesettle
(RNAD)

1890

Saltash

A38

*Royal
Albert
Bridge*

1859

Defiance
Platform
(1905)
[1930]

1859

St Germans
Viaduct

GREAT
WESTERN

Defiance
Halt

WEARDE J

A387

1859

St. Germans

1859

1908

Wivelscombe

Clo 1908

Shillingham Tnl 1908

Wearde
Siding 1859

Cornwall J to Royal Albert Bridge
Mixed Gauge 1876

CORNWALL/
1889 GW
Broad Gauge
Std. G. 1892

A374

Wacker Quay

Scraesdon
Fort

Tregantle Military
Railway

Tregantle Fort

5   4   3   2   1

A

YELVERTON (1885) [1962]

1859
Clo 1962

Clearbrook Halt
(1928) [1962]

1890

**PLYMOUTH, DEVONPORT &
SOUTH WESTERN JUNCTION/
1923 SR**

Shaugh Tnl

B

**PLYMOUTH
AND
DARTMOOR
RAILWAY**

Shaugh Bridge
Platform (1907) [1962]

Beer Ferris /
Bere Ferrers
(1897)

Bickleigh [1962]

**SOUTH DEVON & TAVISTOCK /
1865 SOUTH DEVON /
1878 GW**
Broad Gauge
Mixed Gauge 1876
Std.G 1892

C

Tamerton Foliot
(1897) [1962]

A 386

**LEE MOOR
TRAMWAY**

Cann
Quarry

RAILWAY EXECUTIVE
(1941) ST BUDEAUX J

A 38

[GW] St Budeaux
Platform (1906) /
Ferry Road (1949)

A 3064

Plym Bridge
Platform (1906) [1962]

D

St Budeaux[LSW] /
Victoria Road (1949)

Clo 1962

Weston Mill Halt
(1906) [1921]

Plym Valley
Railway

Marsh Mills
China Clay
Works

Il Point
(RNAD)

1890

Camel's Head Halt
(1906) [1942]

1859

Keyham
(1900)

Clo 1964

Wingfield Villas
Halt (1904)

DEVONPORT J

PLYMOUTH,
NORTH ROAD (1877)

LAIRA J
1848

Marsh Mills (1861) [1962]

Clo 1965
1959

Clo 1965
1965 **BR**

**SOUTH DEVON /
1878 GW**
Broad Gauge
Std.G 1892

E

1   3

Ford / (Devon)
added 1923 [1964]

SD Mixed
Gauge

Laira Green
[1849] /
Laira Halt
(1904) [1930]

Plympton
[1959]

4   8

Mutley
(1871)
[1939]

Lipson Vale
Halt (1904)
[1942] 1849

TAVISTOCK J
SD
Mixed Gauge
1876

5   9

Devonport Tnl
Devonport [GW]
/Albert Road
(1949-1968)

Mutley Tnl

LIPSON J

6   Ford
Tnl

CORN
1859

Lucas Terrace
Halt (1905) [1951]

FRIARY J **GW**

SD
Mixed Gauge 1878

10   *Devonport
Park Tnl*

1876   1876

MOUNT GOULD J

Devonport [LSW]
/King's Road 1949 [1964]

LSW
1859
Clo191

CORNWALL J
PLYMOUTH FRIARY
(1891) [1958]
(1878) (G)

LSW
1878

Mount Gould & Tothill Halt (1905) [1918]

A 38

7   A 374

1886
Clo 1970
LSW

CORN

North Quay
1879

P&D 1892

1898 Clo 1958 **GW**

Stonehouse Pool Quay

1849

1852   1880

CATTE WATER J

Clo 1987   *Cement Works*
1892   **PLYMSTOCK** [1951]

1971
SD
Mixed Gauge 1878

Millbay
Docks

Clo 1950
LSW

*Sutton*Clo 1973
Harbour
Cattewater
Harbour

SD

Clo 1960
1898

Billacombe [1947]

Elburton Cross
[1947]

F

**DEVONPORT
DOCKYARD RAILWAY**
1 Extension
2 Keyham Admiralty Platform
3 Cantilever
4 North Yard
5 Central Office
6 Morice Yard
7 South Yard

**PLYMOUTH /
MILLBAY added
(1877) [1941]**

1879
Clo 1950

GW
Broad Gauge

**P&D /
1883 LSW**

Oreston [1951]

Clo 1961
1897

Bayly's Wharf

TURNCHAPEL
[1951]

Turnchapel Wharves

A 379

**PLYMOUTH &
DARTMOOR /
1923 SR**

Brixton Road
[1947]

8 Ford Platform/Ford Halt
(1906) [1941]
9 Dockyard Halt
(1905)
10 Albert Road Halt
(1906) [1947]

**GREAT
WESTERN**

G

Steer Point [1947]

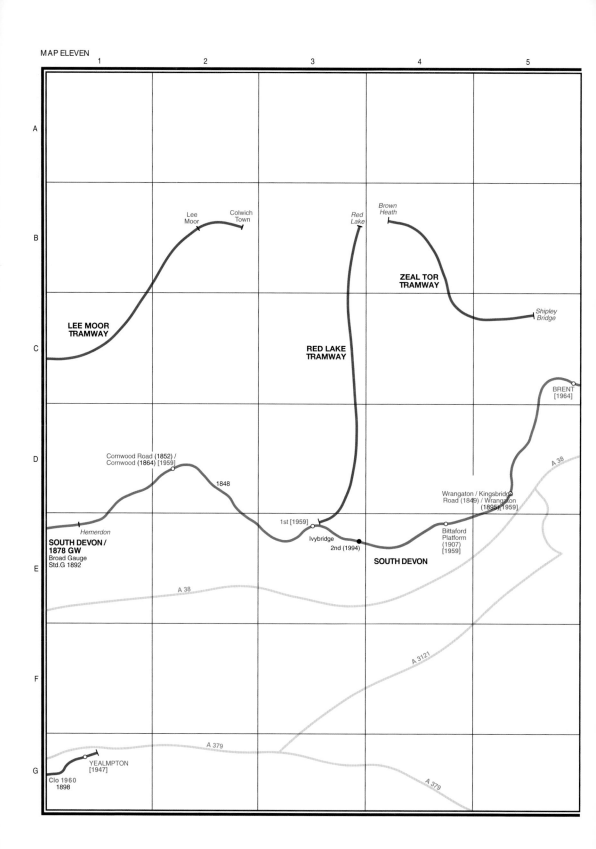

1 2 3 4 5

A

B

Lee Moor

Colwich Town

Red Lake

Brown Heath

ZEAL TOR TRAMWAY

LEE MOOR TRAMWAY

RED LAKE TRAMWAY

Shipley Bridge

C

BRENT [1964]

A 38

D

Cornwood Road (1852) / Cornwood (1864) [1959]

1848

Wrangaton / Kingsbridge Road (1849) / Wrangaton (1895)[1959]

1st [1959]

Hemerdon

SOUTH DEVON / 1878 GW
Broad Gauge
Std.G 1892

Ivybridge
2nd (1994)

Bittaford Platform (1907) [1959]

SOUTH DEVON

E

A 38

F

A 3121

G

A 379

YEALMPTON [1947]

Clo 1960 1898

A 379

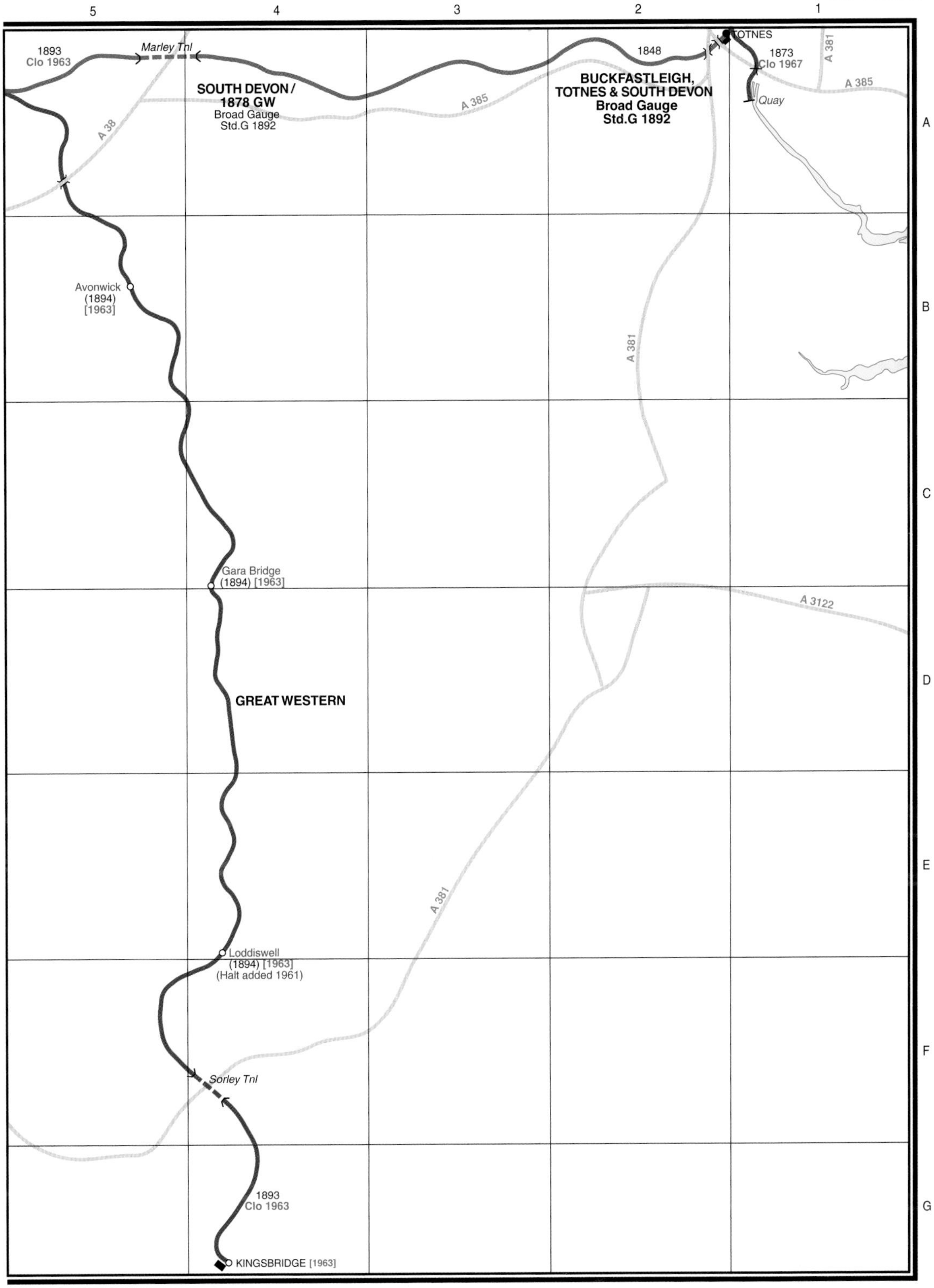

5   4   3   2   1

1893
Clo 1963

Marley Tnl

**SOUTH DEVON /
1878 GW**
Broad Gauge
Std.G 1892

A 385

**BUCKFASTLEIGH,
TOTNES & SOUTH DEVON
Broad Gauge
Std.G 1892**

1848

TOTNES

1873
Clo 1967

A 381

A 385

Quay

A 38

A

Avonwick
(1894)
[1963]

B

A 381

Gara Bridge
(1894) [1963]

C

A 3122

GREAT WESTERN

D

A 381

E

Loddiswell
(1894) [1963]
(Halt added 1961)

A 381

F

Sorley Tnl

1893
Clo 1963

G

KINGSBRIDGE [1963]

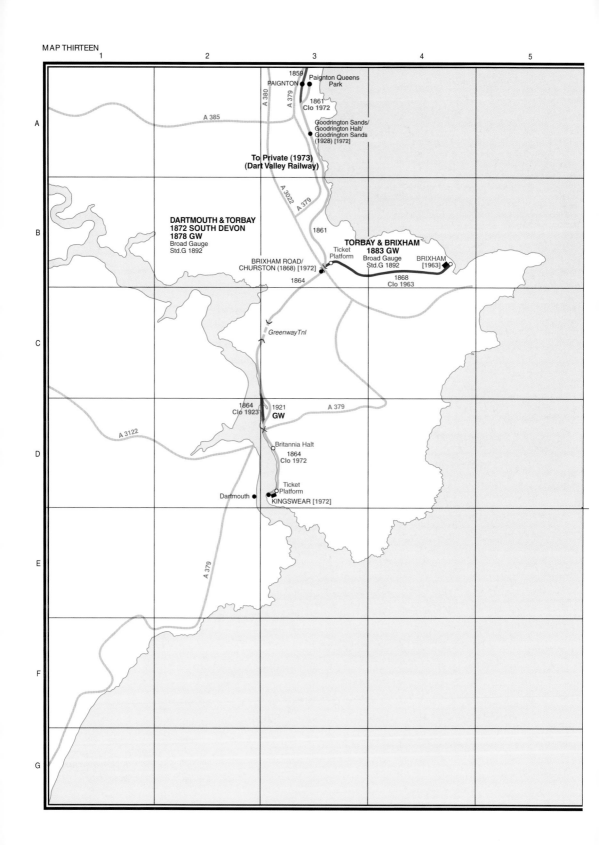

1859
PAIGNTON ● Paignton Queens
Park

A 380
A 379

1861
Clo 1972

Goodrington Sands/
● Goodrington Halt/
● Goodrington Sands
(1928) [1972]

To Private (1973)
(Dart Valley Railway)

A 3022
A 379

DARTMOUTH & TORBAY
1872 SOUTH DEVON
1878 GW
Broad Gauge
Std.G 1892

1861

Ticket   **TORBAY & BRIXHAM**
Platform   **1883 GW**
BRIXHAM ROAD/   Broad Gauge   BRIXHAM
CHURSTON (1868) [1972]   Std.G 1892   [1963] ○

1864   1868
                        Clo 1963

Greenway Tnl

1864   1921
Clo 1923   **GW**   A 379

A 3122

● Britannia Halt
1864
Clo 1972

Ticket
○ Platform
Dartmouth ●
KINGSWEAR [1972]

A 379

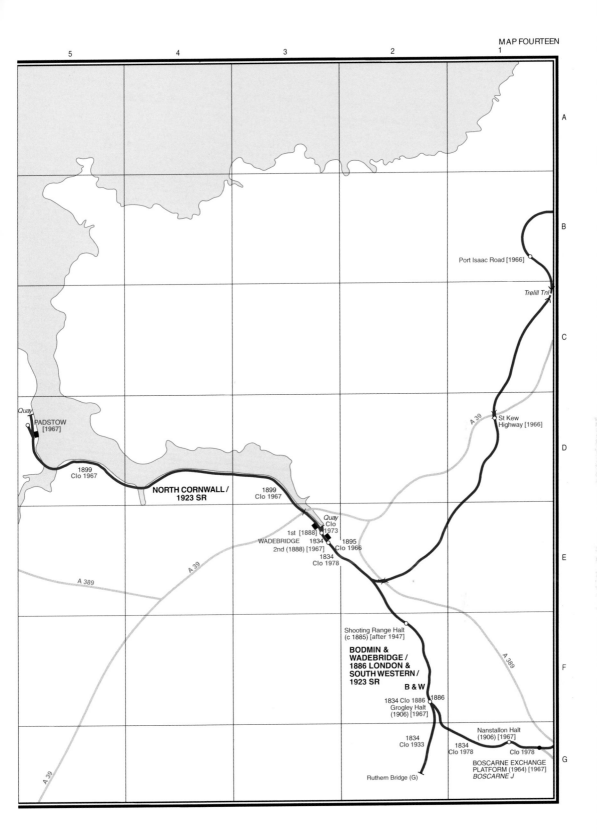

5   4   3   2   1

A

B

Port Isaac Road [1966]

Trelill Tnl

C

Quay

PADSTOW [1967]

A 39   St Kew Highway [1966]

D

1899 Clo 1967

NORTH CORNWALL / 1923 SR

1899 Clo 1967

Quay Clo 1973

1st [1888]

WADEBRIDGE   1834   1895 Clo 1966
2nd (1888) [1967]

1834 Clo 1978

E

A 39

A 389

Shooting Range Halt (c 1885) [after 1947]

BODMIN & WADEBRIDGE / 1886 LONDON & SOUTH WESTERN / 1923 SR

B & W

A 389

F

1834 Clo 1886   1886
Grogley Halt (1906) [1967]

Nanstallon Halt (1906) [1967]

1834 Clo 1933   1834 Clo 1978   Clo 1978

G

A 39

BOSCARNE EXCHANGE PLATFORM (1964) [1967]
BOSCARNE J

Ruthern Bridge (G)

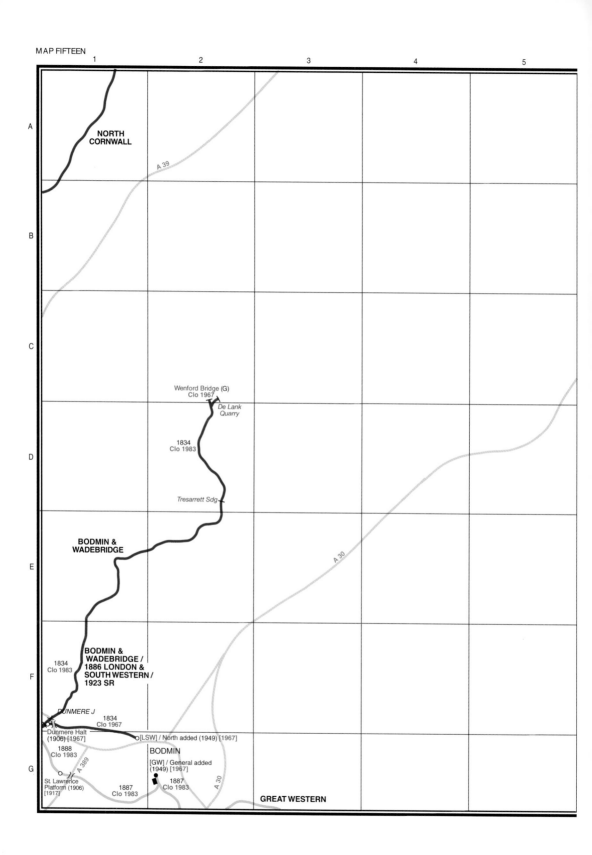

1   2   3   4   5

A

**NORTH
CORNWALL**

A 39

B

C

Wenford Bridge (G)
Clo 1967

*De Lank
Quarry*

1834
Clo 1983

D

Tresarrett Sdg

**BODMIN &
WADEBRIDGE**

A 30

E

**BODMIN &
WADEBRIDGE /
1886 LONDON &
SOUTH WESTERN /
1923 SR**

F

1834
Clo 1983

DUNMERE J

1834
Clo 1967

Dunmere Halt
(1906) [1967]

o[LSW] / North added (1949) [1967]

1888
Clo 1983

BODMIN

A 389

[GW] / General added
(1949) [1967]

G

St. Lawrence
Platform (1906)
[1917]

1887
Clo 1983

1887
Clo 1983

A 30

GREAT WESTERN

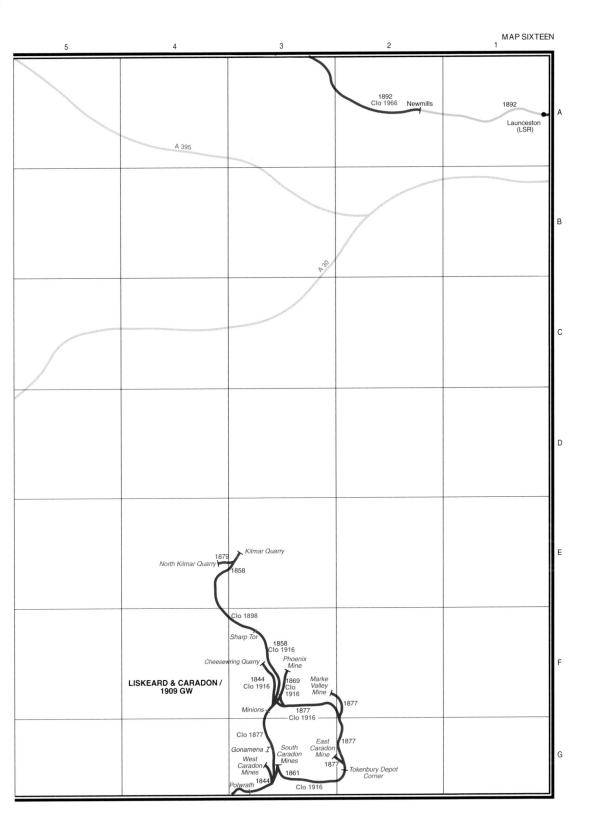

5 4 3 2 1

1892
Clo 1966 Newmills

1892

Launceston
(LSR)

A

A 395

A 30

B

C

D

E

Kilmar Quarry

1879
North Kilmar Quarry
1858

Clo 1898

Sharp Tor

1858
Clo 1916

Cheesewring Quarry

Phoenix
Mine

**LISKEARD & CARADON /
1909 GW**

1844
Clo 1916

1869
Clo
1916

Marke
Valley
Mine

Minions

1877
Clo 1916

1877

F

Clo 1877

East
Caradon
Mine

1877

G

Gonamena

South
Caradon
Mines

West
Caradon
Mines

1877

Tokenbury Depot
Corner

1861

Polwrath

1844

Clo 1916

1 2 3 4 5

A 388

A

[GW]
North
[1952]
Clo 1966

RAILWAY EXECUTIVE
1943 Connection Clo 1966

LAUNCESTON

[LSW]
South
[1966] 1886

A 30

1865
Clo 1966

*Ambrosia
Factory*

Lifton
[1962]

**LAUNCESTON &
SOUTH DEVON /
1874 SOUTH DEVON /
1878 GW
Broad Gauge
Std.G 1892**

B

Coryton
[1962]

C

D

A 388

E

F

**EAST CORNWALL MINERAL/
1894 PLYMOUTH, DEVONPORT
& SOUTH WESTERN JUNCTION/
1923 SR**
3 ft 6 inch Gauge
Std.G 1908

1872
Clo 1966

*Kithill
Quarry*

Cox's Park
Depot (G)(1872)/
Latchley Halt
(1908) [1966]

Seven Stones
Halt (1910) [1917]

Chilsworthy Halt
(1909) [1966]

Clo 1966

*Wheal
Anna
Maria*

Wheal Emma

G

Kellybray (G) 1872 /
CALLINGTON ROAD (1908)/
CALLINGTON (1909) [1966]

Monks Corner
Depot (G)(1872)/
Stoke Climsland
(1908)/ Luckett
(1909) [1966]

Drakewalls Depot (G)(1872)/
1st Gunnislake (1908) [1994]
A 390
Clo 1994
2nd Gunnislake (1994)

**DEVON GREAT
CONSOLS LTD**

**PLYMOUTH, DEVONPORT &
SOUTH WESTERN JUNCTION/
1923 SR**

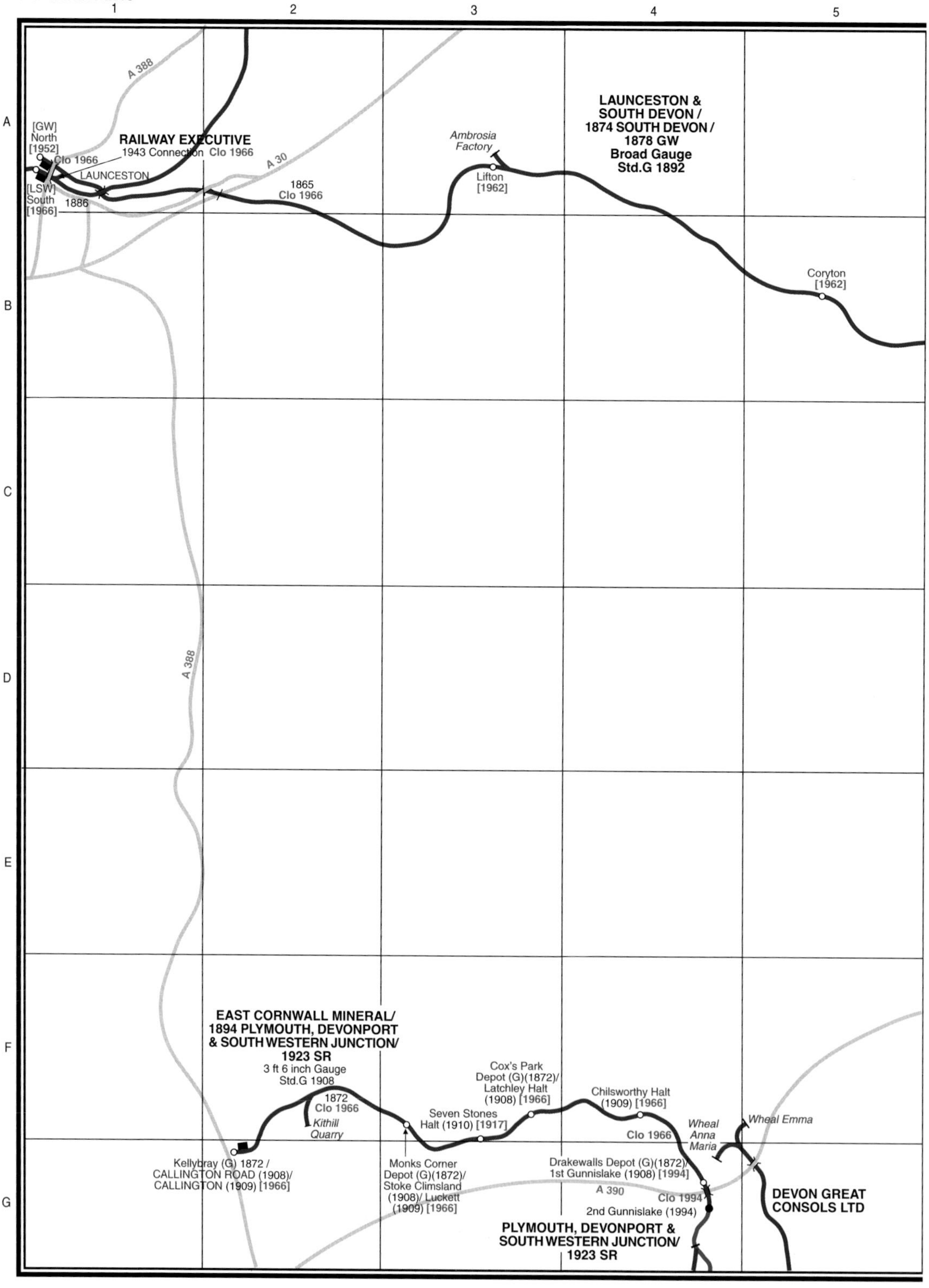

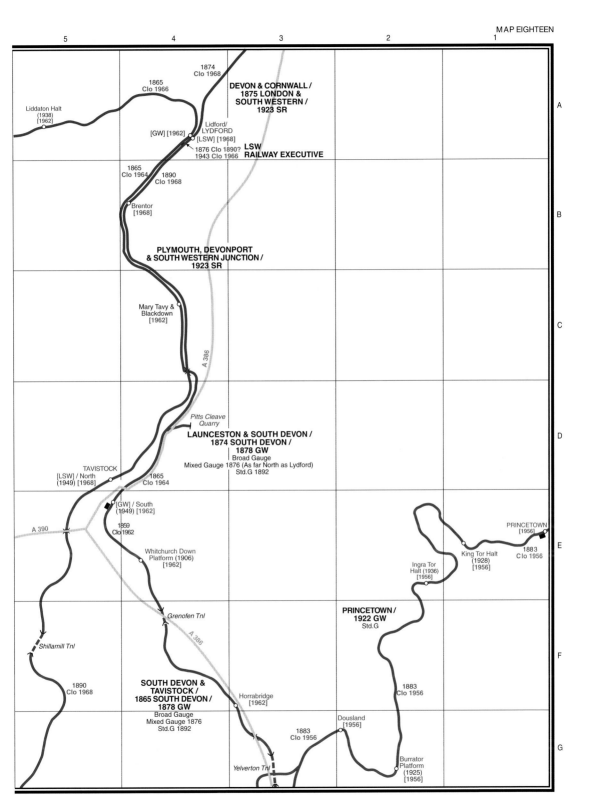

5   4   3   2   1

1874
Clo 1968

1865
Clo 1966

**DEVON & CORNWALL /
1875 LONDON &
SOUTH WESTERN /
1923 SR**

Liddaton Halt
(1938)
[1962]

Lidford/
LYDFORD
[GW] [1962]   [LSW] [1968]

1876 Clo 1890?
1943 Clo 1966

**LSW
RAILWAY EXECUTIVE**

1865
Clo 1964

1890
Clo 1968

Brentor
[1968]

**PLYMOUTH, DEVONPORT
& SOUTH WESTERN JUNCTION /
1923 SR**

Mary Tavy &
Blackdown
[1962]

A 386

Pitts Cleave
Quarry

**LAUNCESTON & SOUTH DEVON /
1874 SOUTH DEVON /
1878 GW**
Broad Gauge
Mixed Gauge 1876 (As far North as Lydford)
Std.G 1892

TAVISTOCK
[LSW] / North
(1949) [1968]

1865
Clo 1964

[GW] / South
(1949) [1962]

1859
Clo 1962

A 390

Whitchurch Down
Platform (1906)
[1962]

PRINCETOWN
[1956]

King Tor Halt
(1928)
[1956]

1883
Clo 1956

Ingra Tor
Halt (1936)
[1956]

Grenofen Tnl

A 386

**PRINCETOWN /
1922 GW**
Std.G

Shillamill Tnl

1890
Clo 1968

**SOUTH DEVON &
TAVISTOCK /
1865 SOUTH DEVON /
1878 GW**
Broad Gauge
Mixed Gauge 1876
Std.G 1892

Horrabridge
[1962]

1883
Clo 1956

1883
Clo 1956

Dousland
[1956]

Burrator
Platform
(1925)
[1956]

Yelverton Tnl

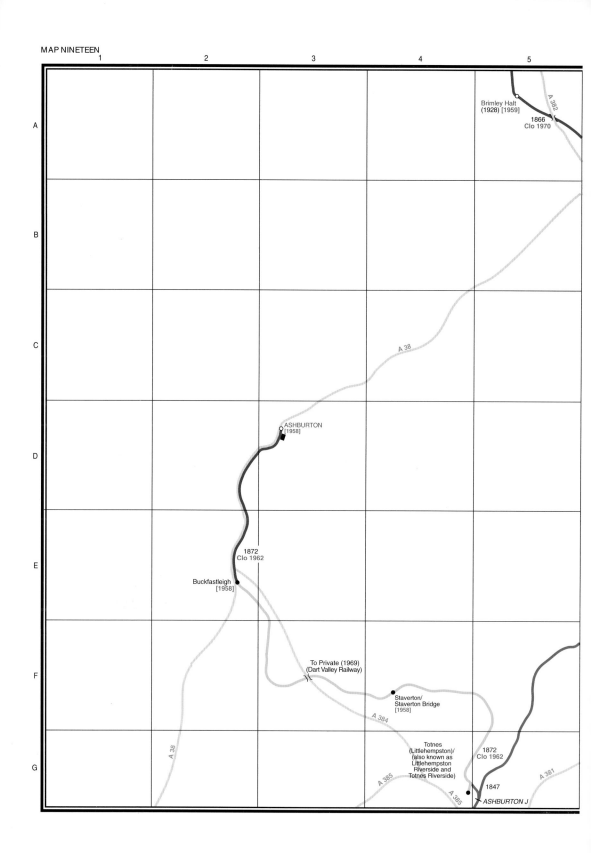

1 2 3 4 5

Brimley Halt
(1928) [1959]
1866
Clo 1970

A 382

A

B

C

A 38

ASHBURTON
[1958]

D

1872
Clo 1962

E

Buckfastleigh
[1958]

To Private (1969)
(Dart Valley Railway)

F

Staverton/
Staverton Bridge
[1958]

A 384

A 38

Totnes
(Littlehempston)/
(also known as
Littlehempston
Riverside and
Totnes Riverside)

1872
Clo 1962

A 381

G

A 385

A 385

1847
ASHBURTON J

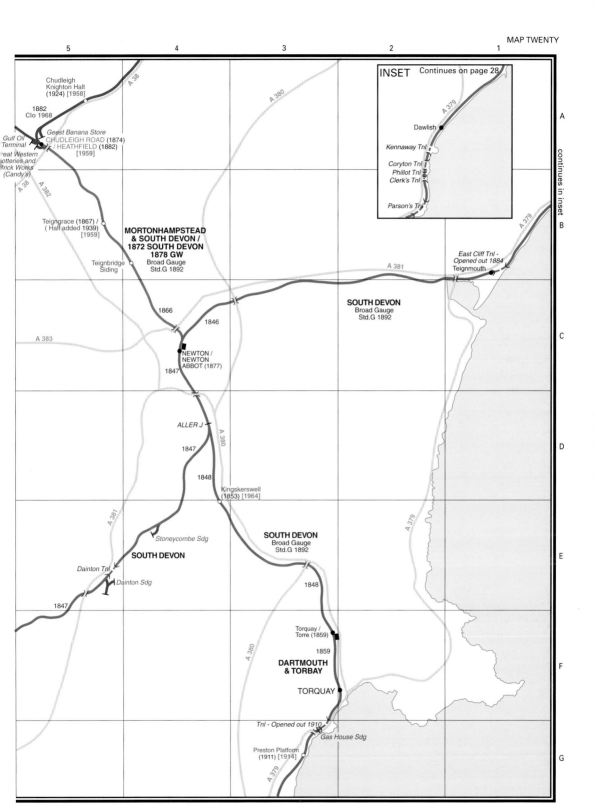

5   4   3   2   1

A 38
A 380

INSET Continues on page 28

A 379

Dawlish

Kennaway Tnl

Coryton Tnl
Phillot Tnl
Clerk's Tnl

Parson's Tnl

continues in inset

Chudleigh
Knighton Halt
(1924) [1958]

1882
Clo 1968

Gulf Oil
Terminal
Geest Banana Store
CHUDLEIGH ROAD (1874)
/ HEATHFIELD (1882)
[1959]

Great Western
Potteries and
Brick Works
(Candy's)

A 38
A 382

Teigngrace (1867) /
(Halt added 1939)
[1959]

**MORTONHAMPSTEAD
& SOUTH DEVON /
1872 SOUTH DEVON
1878 GW**
Broad Gauge
Std.G 1892

Teignbridge
Siding

A 381

A 379

East Cliff Tnl -
Opened out 1884
Teignmouth

SOUTH DEVON
Broad Gauge
Std.G 1892

A 38

A 383

1866

1846

NEWTON /
NEWTON
ABBOT (1877)

1847

ALLER J

A 380

1847

1848

Kingskerswell
(1853) [1964]

SOUTH DEVON
Broad Gauge
Std.G 1892

A 379

A 381

Stoneycombe Sdg

SOUTH DEVON

Dainton Tnl
Dainton Sdg

1847

A 380

1848

Torquay /
Torre (1859)

1859

**DARTMOUTH
& TORBAY**

TORQUAY

Tnl - Opened out 1910

Gas House Sdg

Preston Platform
(1911) [1914]

A 379

A   B   C   D   E   F   G

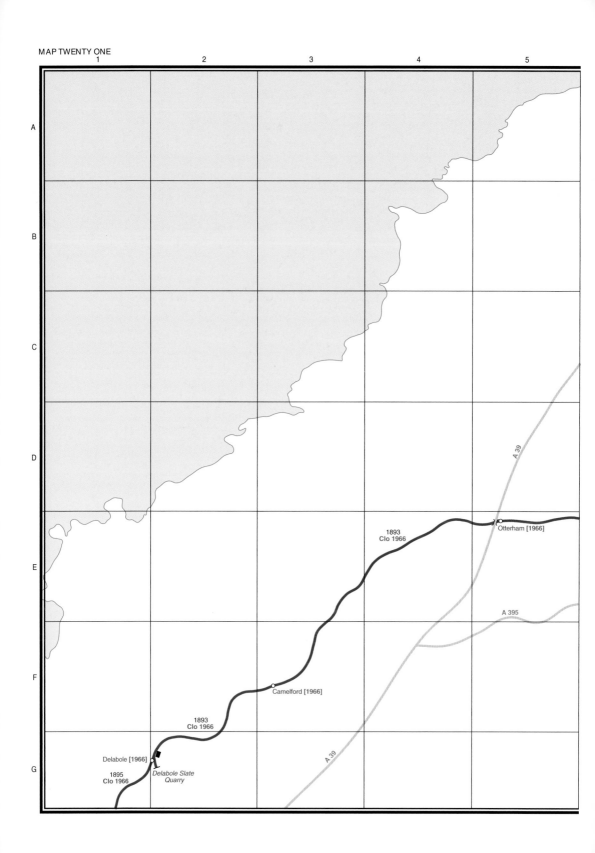

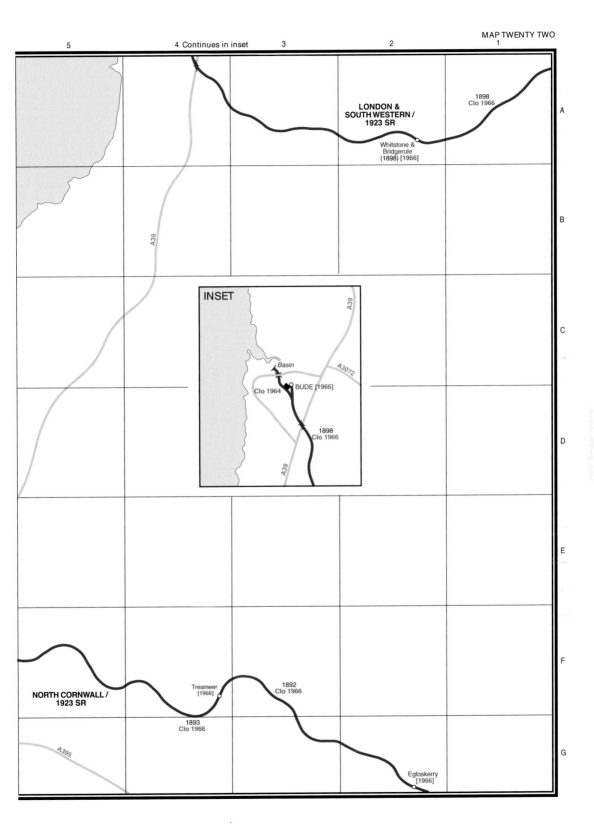

5   4 Continues in inset   3   2   1

**LONDON &
SOUTH WESTERN /
1923 SR**

1898
Clo 1966

A

Whitstone &
Bridgerule
(1898) [1966]

A39

B

INSET

A39

Basin

A3072

Clo 1964   BUDE [1966]

1898
Clo 1966

A39

C

D

E

**NORTH CORNWALL /
1923 SR**

Tresmeer
[1966]

1892
Clo 1966

F

1893
Clo 1966

A395

Egloskerry
[1966]

G

1   2   3   4   5

A3072   Holsworthy   1879
1898   1st (1879)   2nd (1898)   **LONDON & SOUTH**
[1898]   [1966]   **WESTERN**

A3072

A ○ Dunsland Cross
[1966]

1879
Clo 1966

A3079

B

1886
Clo 1966

C

NORTH CORNWALL /
1923 SR

A388   ○ Ashwater
D   [1966]

E

○ Tower Hill
[1966]
F

1886
Clo 1966

A30
G

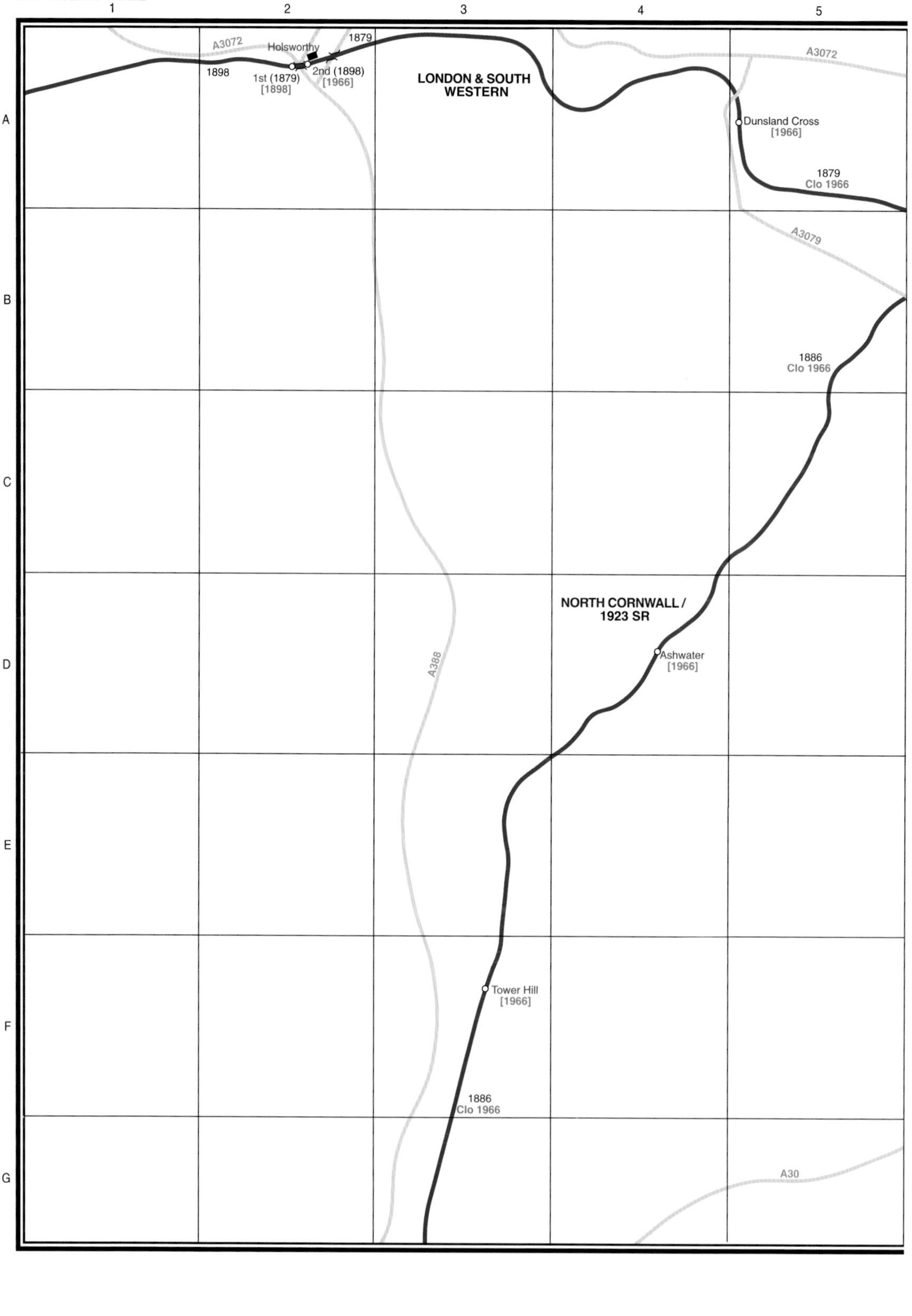

5 4 3 2 1

1879
Clo 1966

1925
Clo 1965

1886
Clo 1966

A

HALWILL & BEAWORTHY /
HALWILL JUNCTION (1887) /
HALWILL (1923) [1966]

1879
Clo1966

**LONDON &
SOUTH WESTERN /
1923 SR**

B

Ashbury/ Ashbury & North Lew/
Ashbury for North Lew/
Ashbury [1966]

A3079

C

Maddaford Moor
Halt (1926)
[1966]

1879
Clo 1966

A386

A30

D

MELDON J

A30

**DEVON &
CORNWALL**

E

1874
Clo 1968

Bridestowe
[1968]

F

A386

**DEVON & CORNWALL /
1875 LONDON & SOUTH WESTERN /
1923 SR**

1874
Clo 1968

G

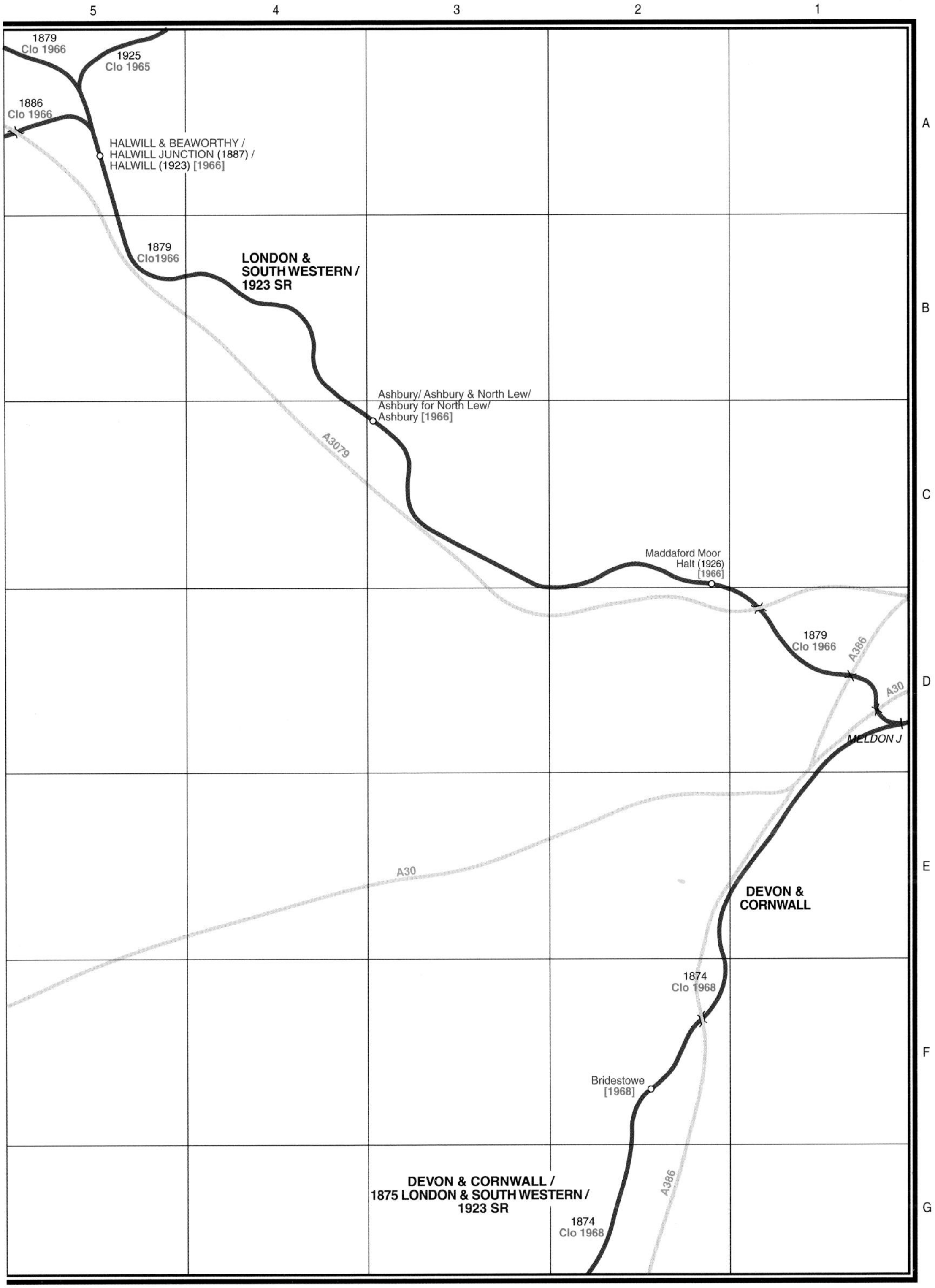

1   2   3   4   5

A3072

A3124

A3072

A

1867   1865

North
Tawton
[1972]

Okehampton Road /
Belstone Corner (1871) /   1867
Sampford Courtenay (1872) [1972]

1871

B

A386

A3124

DARTMOOR
RAILWAY
(PRIVATE)

DEVON & CORNWALL /
1875 LONDON &
SOUTH WESTERN /
1923 SR

C

A30

1871

1874   OKEHAMPTON
[1972]

Clo 1994

D

Meldon Quarry
Clo 1968

E

F

G

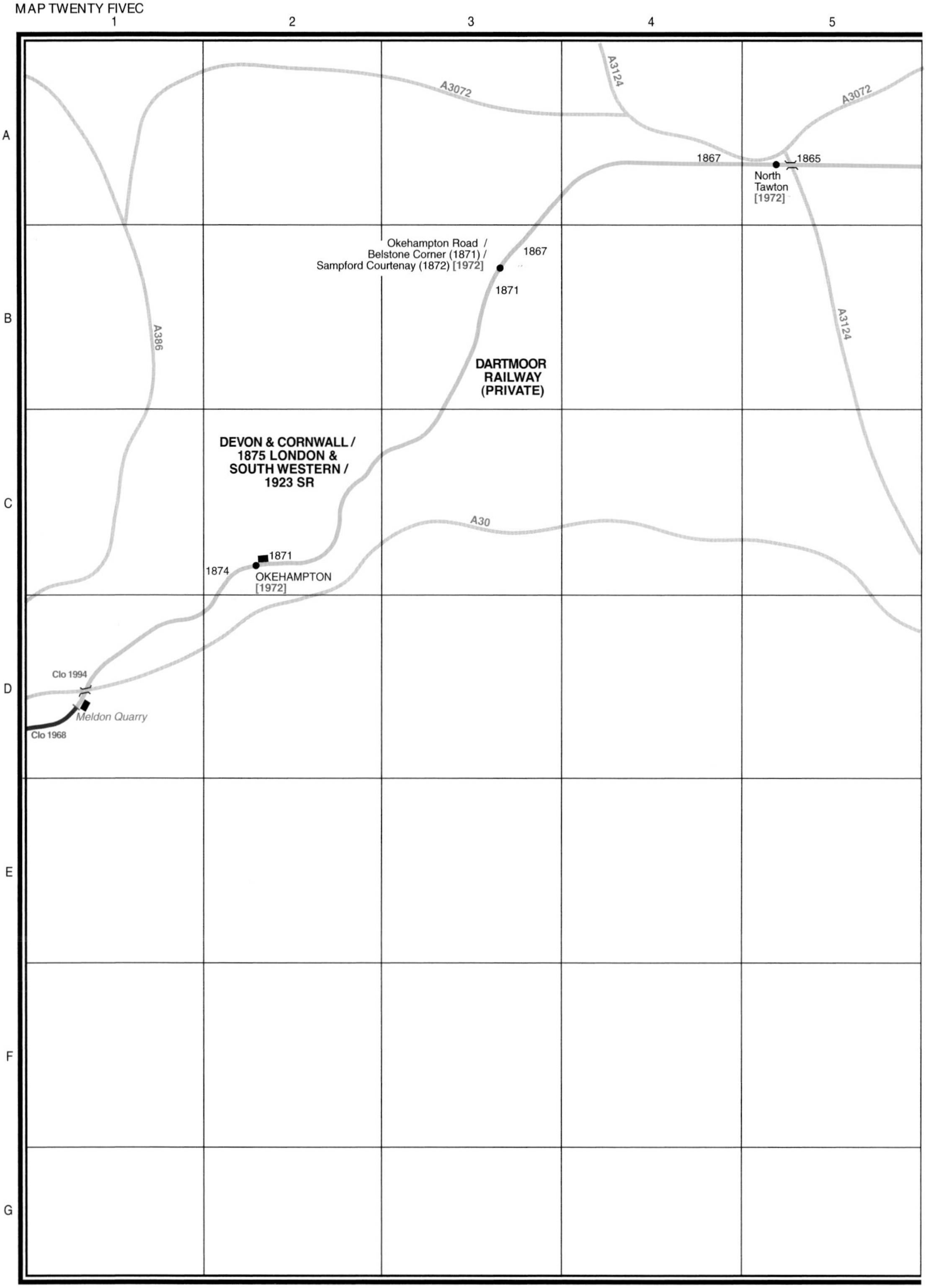

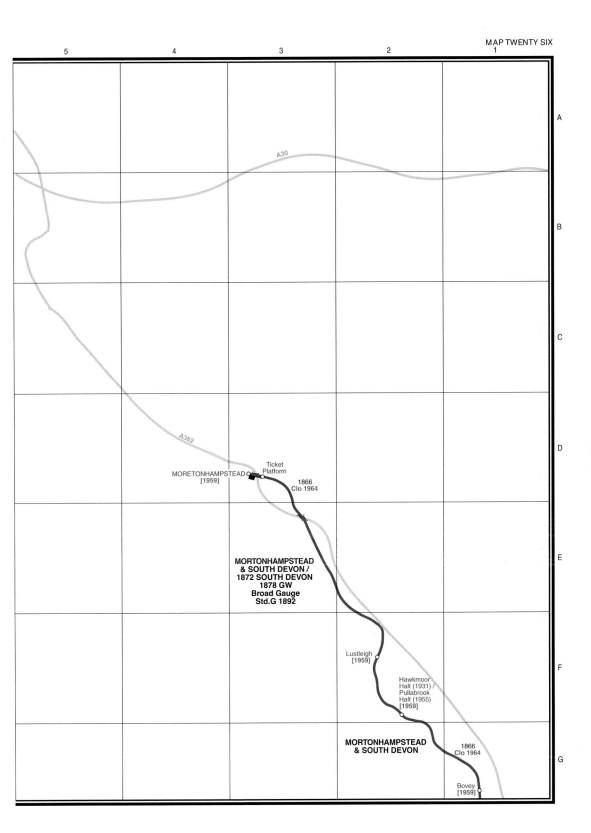

5   4   3   2   1

A

A30

B

C

A382

D

Ticket
Platform

MORETONHAMPSTEAD
[1959]

1866
Clo 1964

MORTONHAMPSTEAD
& SOUTH DEVON /
1872 SOUTH DEVON
1878 GW
Broad Gauge
Std.G 1892

E

Lustleigh
[1959]

F

Hawkmoor
Halt (1931) /
Pullabrook
Halt (1955)
[1959]

MORTONHAMPSTEAD
& SOUTH DEVON

1866
Clo 1964

G

Bovey
[1959]

1   2   3   4   5

Mixed Gauge 1862

Mount Pleasant
Road Halt (1906)
[1928]

Whipton Bridge
Halt
(1906) [1923]

**BRISTOL &
EXETER**

Lions Holt
Halt (1906) /
St James Park
Halt (1946)

EXMOUTH J

1860

LSW

A

1844

1860

*Black Boy
Tnl*

Polsloe Bridge
Halt

1861

ST DAVIDS

*St Davids
Tnl*

Ticket
Platform

Polsloe Bridge
(1907)

1846

1862

QUEEN STREET
/ CENTRAL (1933)

LSW

SOUTH DEVON

LSW   EX

Mixed Gauge

1904
Clo 1983

SD

1867
Clo 1983

EXETER

St Thomas/Exeter/St
Thomas/ Exeter
St Thomas

Mixed Gauge
1871

1   Electricity Works
2   Basin
3   Gas Works
4   Oil Depot
5   Marsh Barton Scrap Yard
6   Cadbury Fry
7   Kings Asphalt
8   Alphington Road Goods
9   Cattle Market

B

2

CITY
BASIN J

1

3

7

1903
Clo 1992

8

4

5

**EXETER /
1923 GW**

6

Marsh
Barton

9

Ide
[1958]

Alphington Halt
(1928) [1958]

Longdown
[1958]

*Longdown
(Perridge)
Tnl*

**SOUTH DEVON /
1878 GW**

Clo 1958

Culver Tnl

Broad Gauge
Std.G 1892

C

**EXETER /
1923 GW**

Dunsford Halt
(1928) [1958]

1846

M5

1903
Clo 1958

Teign House (G)
(1882)/
Christow
(1903) [1958]

Exminster (1852)
[1964]

Baryles Mine
Bridford Bay/
Quarry (1910)
[1931]

D

1882
Clo 1961

**TEIGN
VALLEY /
1923 GW
Std.G**

Ashton
[1958]

E

*Whetcombe
Sdg*

Clo 1961

Trusham [1958]

Clo 1965

F

Crockham Sdg

Clo 1968

TEIGN VALLEY

G

Chudleigh [1958]

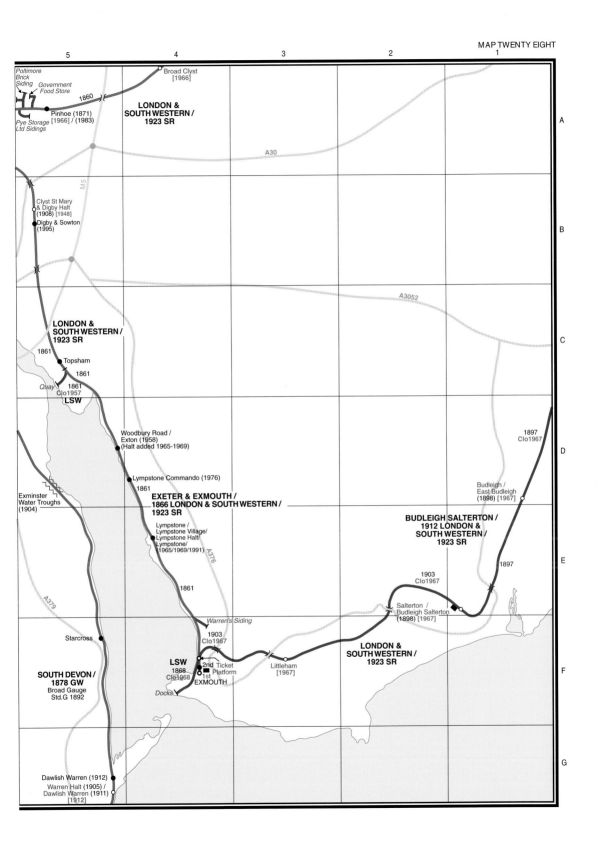

5   4   3   2   1

Poltimore
Brick
Siding
Government
Food Store
1860
Pinhoe (1871)
Pye Storage [1966] / (1983)
Ltd Sidings

Broad Clyst
[1966]

**LONDON &
SOUTH WESTERN /
1923 SR**

A30

M5

Clyst St Mary
& Digby Halt
(1908) [1948]
Digby & Sowton
(1995)

A3052

**LONDON &
SOUTH WESTERN /
1923 SR**

A   B   C   D   E   F   G

1861
Topsham
1861
Quay   1861
Clo1957
LSW

Woodbury Road /
Exton (1958)
(Halt added 1965-1969)

Lympstone Commando (1976)
1861

1897
Clo1967

**EXETER & EXMOUTH /
1866 LONDON & SOUTH WESTERN /
1923 SR**

Exminster
Water Troughs
(1904)

Lympstone /
Lympstone Village /
Lympstone Halt /
Lympstone /
(1965/1969/1991)

Budleigh /
East Budleigh
(1898) [1967]

**BUDLEIGH SALTERTON /
1912 LONDON &
SOUTH WESTERN /
1923 SR**

1861

A379

1861

Warren's Siding

1903
Clo1967

1903
Clo1967

1897

Salterton /
Budleigh Salterton
(1898) [1967]

Starcross

**LONDON &
SOUTH WESTERN /
1923 SR**

LSW
1868
Clo1968
2nd   Ticket
Platform
1st
EXMOUTH

Littleham
[1967]

Docks

**SOUTH DEVON /
1878 GW**
Broad Gauge
Std.G 1892

Dawlish Warren (1912)
Warren Halt (1905) /
Dawlish Warren (1911)
[1912]

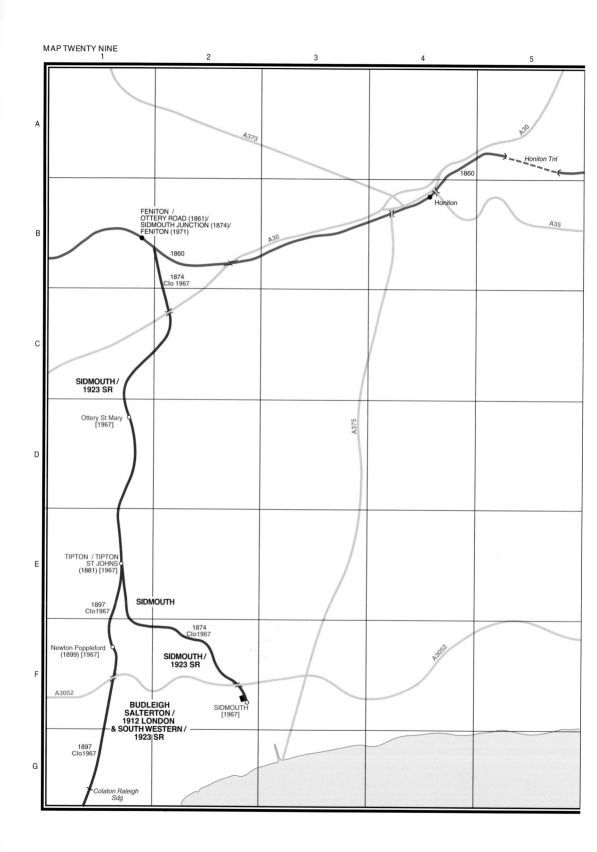

1   2   3   4   5

A

A373

A30

Honiton Tnl

1860

B

FENITON /
OTTERY ROAD (1861)/
SIDMOUTH JUNCTION (1874)/
FENITON (1971)

Honiton

A35

A30

1860

1874
Clo 1967

C

SIDMOUTH /
1923 SR

A375

Ottery St Mary
[1967]

D

E

TIPTON / TIPTON
ST JOHNS
(1881) [1967]

1897
Clo1967

SIDMOUTH

1874
Clo1967

Newton Poppleford
(1899) [1967]

SIDMOUTH /
1923 SR

A3052

F

A3052

BUDLEIGH
SALTERTON /
1912 LONDON
& SOUTH WESTERN /
1923 SR

SIDMOUTH
[1967]

1897
Clo1967

G

Colaton Raleigh
Sdg

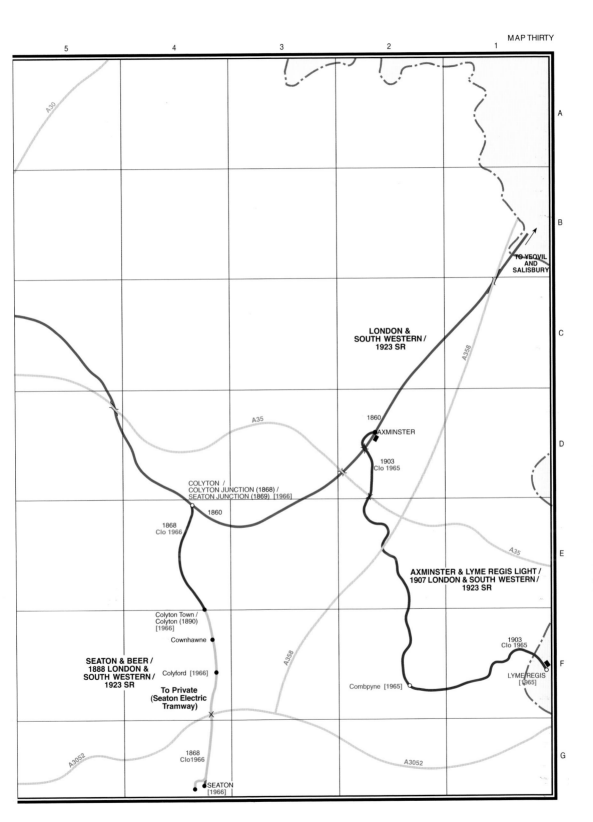

5   4   3   2   1

A

A30

B

TO YEOVIL
AND
SALISBURY

LONDON &
SOUTH WESTERN /
1923 SR

C

A358

A35

1860

AXMINSTER

D

1903
Clo 1965

COLYTON /
COLYTON JUNCTION (1868) /
SEATON JUNCTION (1869) [1966]

1860

1868
Clo 1966

E

A35

AXMINSTER & LYME REGIS LIGHT /
1907 LONDON & SOUTH WESTERN /
1923 SR

Colyton Town /
Colyton (1890)
[1966]

Cownhawne

1903
Clo 1965

SEATON & BEER /
1888 LONDON &
SOUTH WESTERN /
1923 SR

Colyford [1966]

A358

F

LYME REGIS
[1965]

To Private
(Seaton Electric
Tramway)

Combpyne [1965]

A3052

A3052

G

1868
Clo1966

SEATON
[1966]

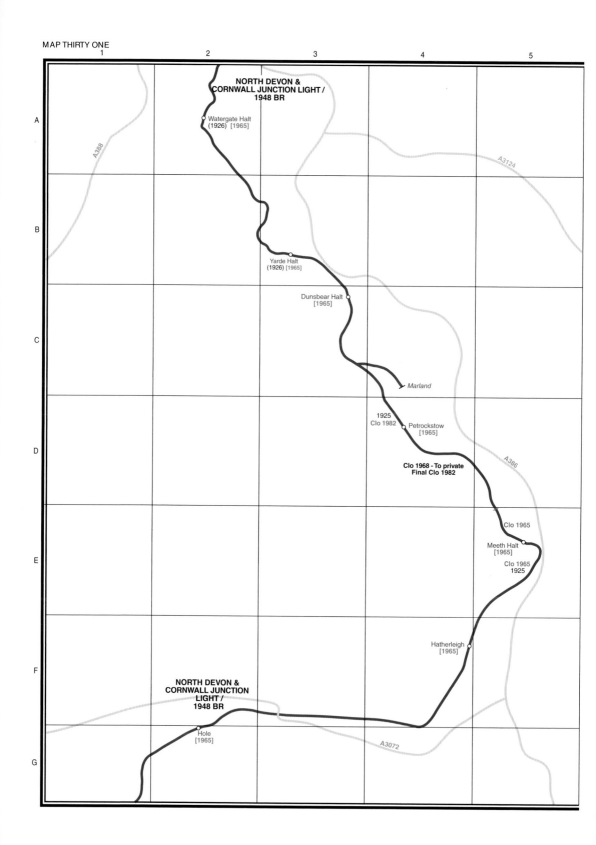

**NORTH DEVON &
CORNWALL JUNCTION LIGHT /
1948 BR**

Watergate Halt
(1926) [1965]

Yarde Halt
(1926) [1965]

Dunsbear Halt
[1965]

Marland

1925
Clo 1982   Petrockstow
[1965]

Clo 1968 - To private
Final Clo 1982

Clo 1965

Meeth Halt
[1965]

Clo 1965
1925

Hatherleigh
[1965]

**NORTH DEVON &
CORNWALL JUNCTION
LIGHT /
1948 BR**

Hole
[1965]

A388

A3124

A396

A3072

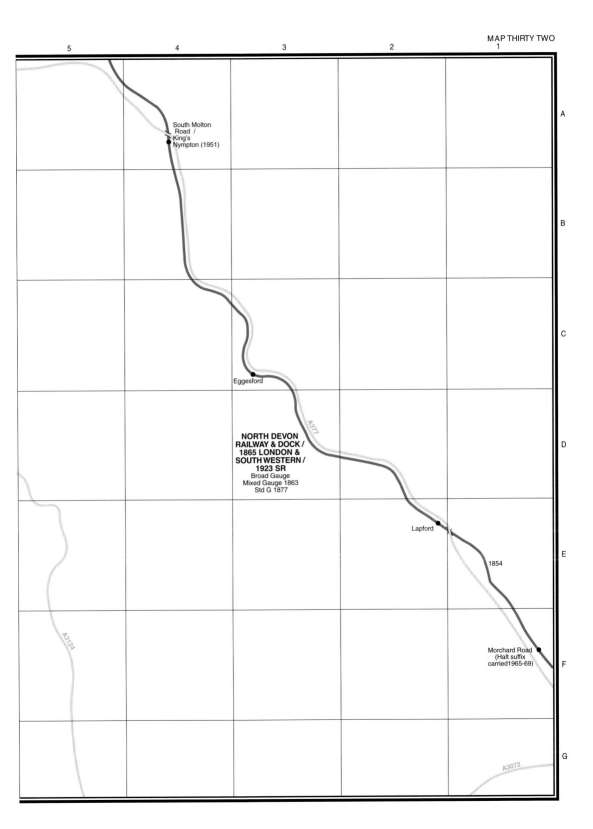

5   4   3   2   1

A

South Molton
Road /
King's
Nympton (1951)

B

C

Eggesford

A377

**NORTH DEVON
RAILWAY & DOCK /
1865 LONDON &
SOUTH WESTERN /
1923 SR**
Broad Gauge
Mixed Gauge 1863
Std G 1877

D

Lapford

E

1854

A3124

Morchard Road
(Halt suffix
carried1965-69)

F

A3072

G

1 2 3 4 5

A

Morchard Road
(Halt suffix carried
(1965-69)

**NORTH DEVON
RAILWAY & DOCK /
1865 LONDON &
SOUTH WESTERN /
1923 SR
Broad Gauge
Mixed Gauge 1863
Std G 1877**

A377

● Copplestone

B

A3072

A377

1865
Clo 1994

1854

Bow
[1972]

● COLEFORD J

**To Private (1994)
(Dartmoor Railway)**

1854

C

1854

Yeoford Junction/
Yeoford

**NORTH DEVON
RAIL WAY & DOCK**

D

E

A30

F

A382

G

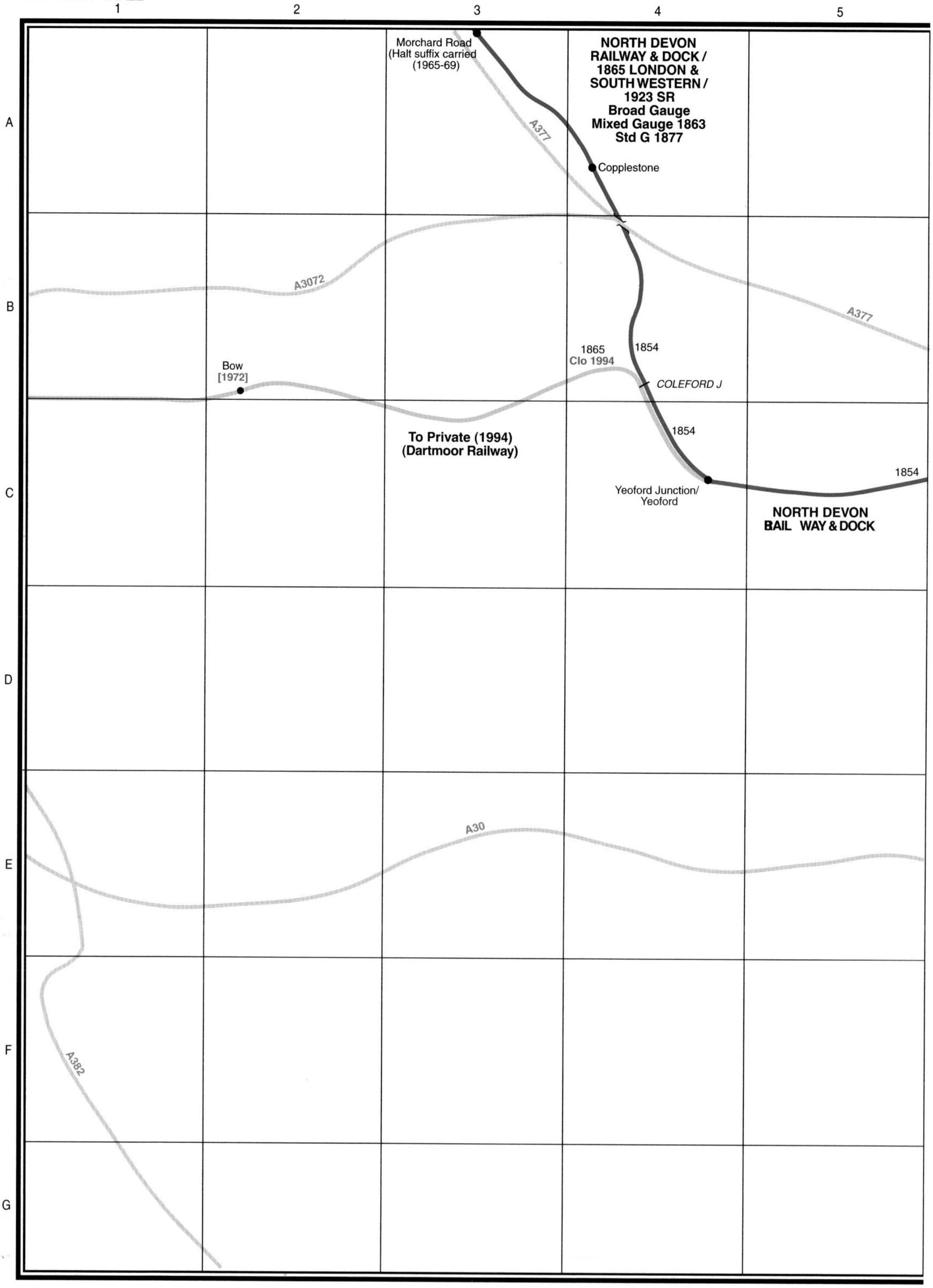

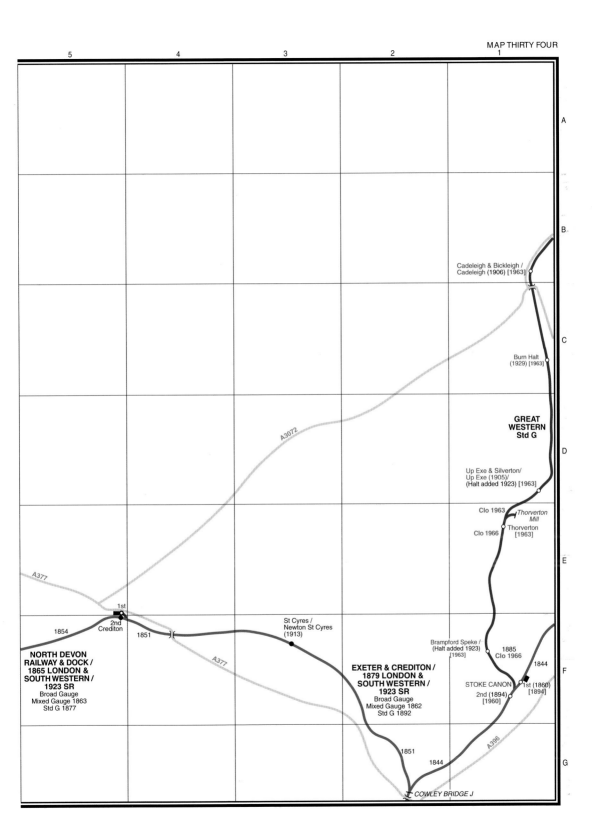

5   4   3   2   1

A

B

Cadeleigh & Bickleigh /
Cadeleigh (1906) [1963]

C

Burn Halt
(1929) [1963]

**GREAT
WESTERN
Std G**

A3072

D

Up Exe & Silverton/
Up Exe (1905)/
(Halt added 1923) [1963]

Clo 1963   Thorverton
Mill
Clo 1966   Thorverton
[1963]

E

A377

1st

2nd
Crediton

1854

1851

A377

St Cyres /
Newton St Cyres
(1913)

**NORTH DEVON
RAILWAY & DOCK /
1865 LONDON &
SOUTH WESTERN /
1923 SR**
Broad Gauge
Mixed Gauge 1863
Std G 1877

**EXETER & CREDITON /
1879 LONDON &
SOUTH WESTERN /
1923 SR**
Broad Gauge
Mixed Gauge 1862
Std G 1892

Brampford Speke /
(Halt added 1923)
[1963]

1885
Clo 1966

1844

STOKE CANON   1st (1860)
2nd (1894)   [1894]
[1960]

F

1851

1844

A396

COWLEY BRIDGE J

G

1   2   3   4   5

A

West Exe
Halt (1928)
[1963]
1885 Clo1963

A396

Halberton Halt
(1927) [1964]

BRISTOL
& EXETER /
1876 GW
Broad Gauge
Std.G 1884

1844

Park Sdg

1848
Clo 1967

1876
Clo 1975

TIVERTON ROAD/
TIVERTON JUNCTION
(1848) [1986]

Coldharbour Halt
(1929) [1963]

CULM VALLEY LIGHT /
1880 GW
Std.G

1844

B

Cullompton
[1964]

1844

C

A373

BRISTOL & EXETER

D

A396

M5

Hele & Bradninch
[1964]

BRISTOL & EXETER /
1876 GW
Broad Gauge
Mixed Gauge 1876
Std G 1892

Silverton
(1867)
[1964]

E

Bridge Paper
Mill

F

Whimple

G

LONDON &
SOUTH WESTERN /
1923 SR

Broad Clyst Permanent
Way Depot

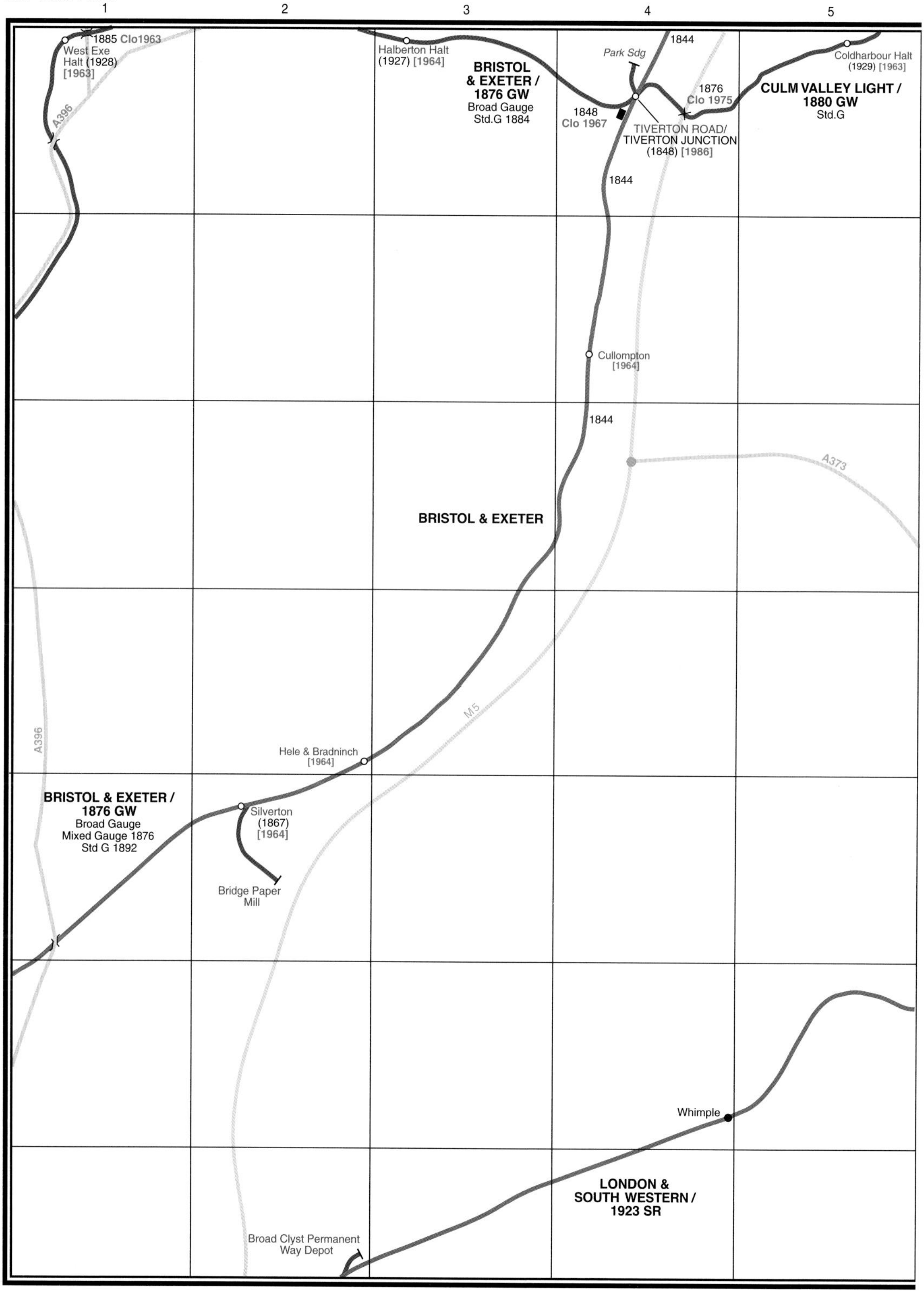

5   4   3   2   1

A

**TO TAUNTON
AND
BRISTOL**

Whiteball Tnl

B

Westleigh   Burlescombe
(1867) [1964]

**WESTLEIGH
MINERAL RAILWAY**

**BRISTOL & EXETER /
1876 GW**
Broad Gauge
Mixed Gauge 1876
Std.G 1892

M5

A38

C

*Culm Valley
Dairy*

Whitehall Halt
(1933) [1963]

Culmstock
[1963]

HEMYOCK
[1963]

Uffculme
[1963]

**CULM VALLEY LIGHT /
1880 GW**
Std.G

D

Coldharbour Halt
(1929) [1963]

E

F

A373

G

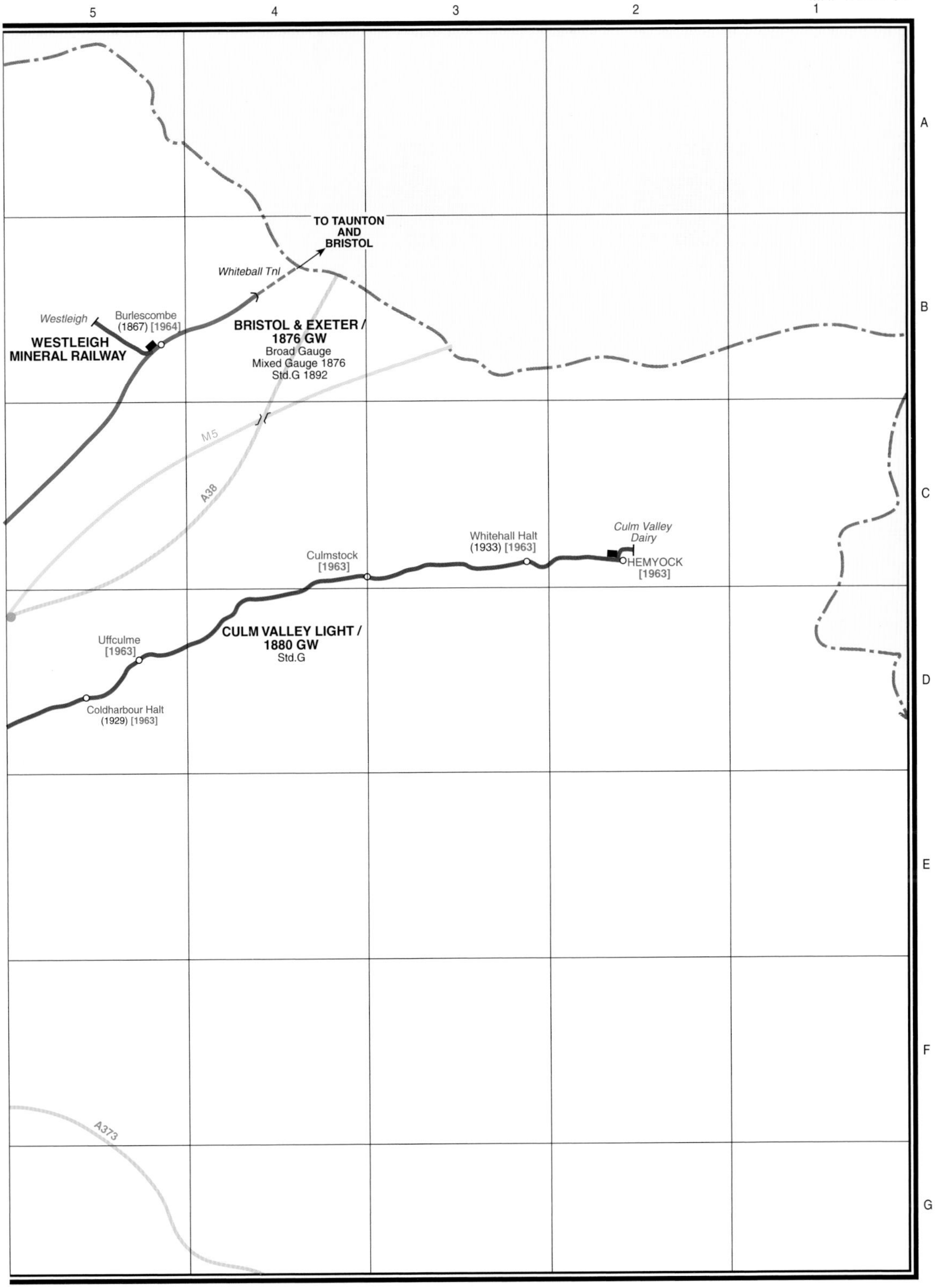

Wrafton
[1970]

Quay

1855
Clo 1982

Fremington
(1848) [1965]

1848
Clo 1982

East Yelland
Power Station

**TAW VALE RAILWAY & DOCK /
1851 NORTH DEVON
RAIWAY & DOCK /
1865 LONDON &
SOUTH WESTERN /
1923 SR**
Std. G
Broad Gauge 1855
Mixed Gauge 1863
Std. G 1877

APPLEDORE

1908

Richmond
Road Halt

Lover's
Lane Halt

Instow [1965]

**BIDEFORD EXTENSION /
1865 LONDON & SOUTH WESTERN /
1923 SR**
Broad Gauge
Mixed Gauge 1864
Std. G 1877

Beach
Road
Halt

1901

1908
Northam

Westward Ho!

**BIDEFORD,
WESTWARD HO!
& APPLEDORE**
Line and All Stations
Clo 1917

1855
Clo 1982

Clo 1982

Cornborough Cliffe
Halt (after 1910)

1901

Causeway
Crossing Halt

The Lane
Halt

Abbotsham Road

Kenwith Castle
Halt (1902)

Bideford (Yard)
Halt
Strand Road
Halt

1901

Quay

1855

1st [1872]

1872

BIDEFORD

2nd [1965]

**LONDON &
SOUTH WESTERN /
1923 SR**

Clo 1982

**NORTH DEVON &
CORNWALL JUNCTION LIGHT /
1948 BR**

Torrington [1965]

1925

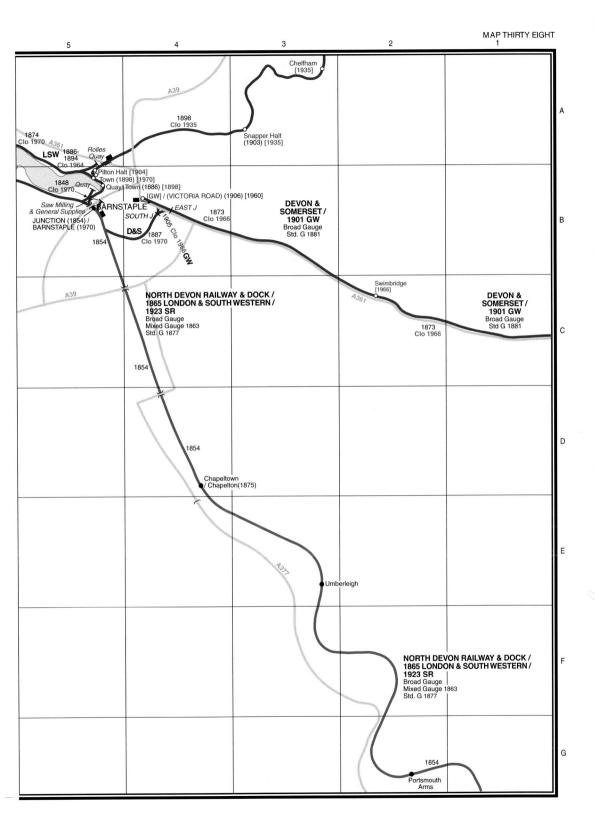

Chelfham
[1935]

1898
Clo 1935

Snapper Halt
(1903) [1935]

1874
Clo 1970

LSW

1886-
1894
Clo 1964

Rolles
Quay

Pilton Halt [1904]
Town (1898) [1970]
Quay Town (1886) [1898]

1848
Clo 1970

Quay

[GW] / (VICTORIA ROAD) (1906) [1960]

Saw Milling
& General Supplies

JUNCTION (1854) /
BARNSTAPLE (1970)

BARNSTAPLE

SOUTH J

EAST J

1873
Clo 1966

DEVON &
SOMERSET /
1901 GW
Broad Gauge
Std. G 1881

D&S

1887
Clo 1970

1905 Clo 1966 GW

1854

NORTH DEVON RAILWAY & DOCK /
1865 LONDON & SOUTH WESTERN /
1923 SR
Broad Gauge
Mixed Gauge 1863
Std. G 1877

Swimbridge
[1966]

1873
Clo 1966

DEVON &
SOMERSET /
1901 GW
Broad Gauge
Std G 1881

1854

1854

Chapeltown
/ Chapelton (1875)

Umberleigh

NORTH DEVON RAILWAY & DOCK /
1865 LONDON & SOUTH WESTERN /
1923 SR
Broad Gauge
Mixed Gauge 1863
Std. G 1877

1854

Portsmouth
Arms

1 2 3 4 5

A

A399

B

**DEVON & SOMERSET /
1901 GW**
Broad Gauge
Std G 1881

A361

C

Castle Hill / Filleigh
(1881) [1966]

Castle Hill Tnl

1873
Clo 1966

DEVON & SOMERSET

South Molton
[1966]

D

Molland/
Bishop's Nympton
& Molland
(1876) [1966]

A361

E

F

G

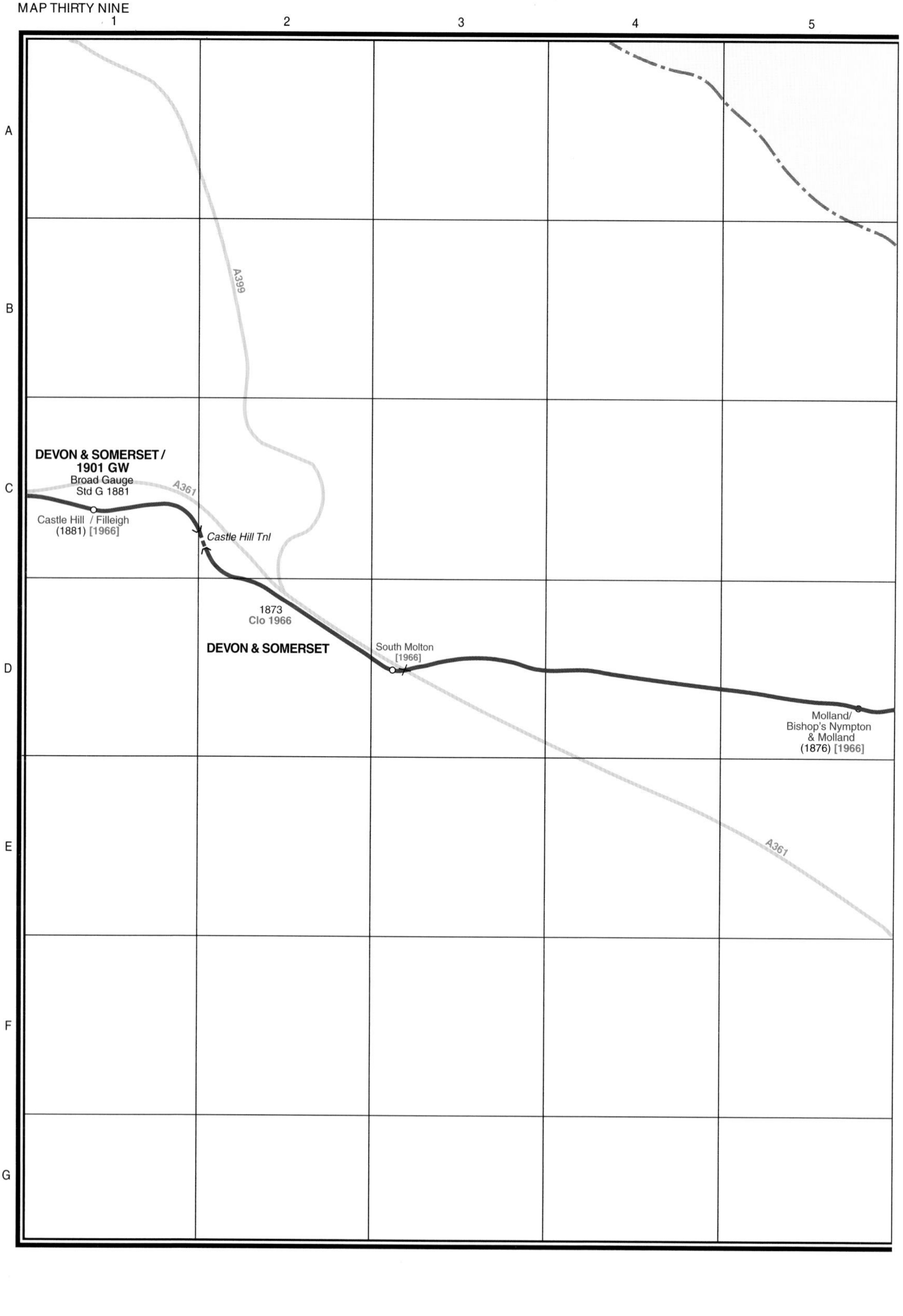

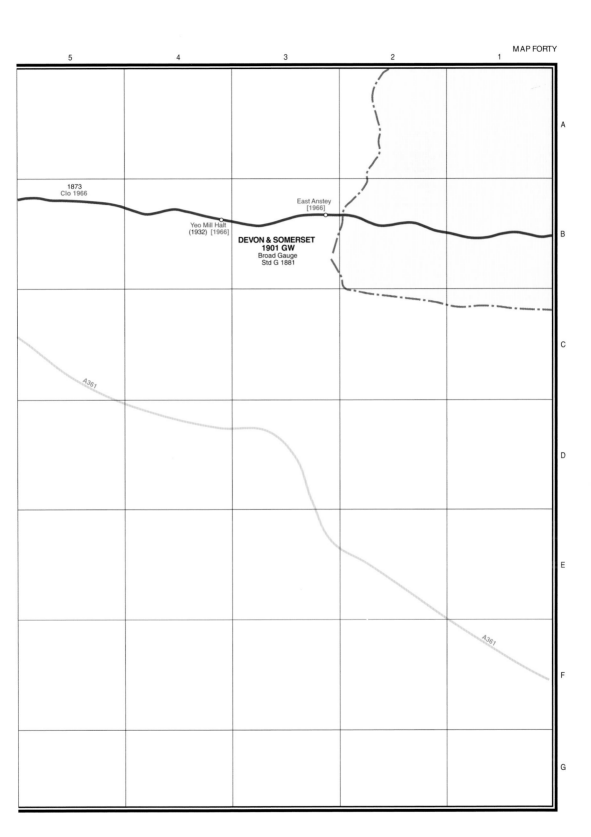

5   4   3   2   1

A

1873
Clo 1966

East Anstey
[1966]

Yeo Mill Halt
(1932) [1966]

**DEVON & SOMERSET
1901 GW**
Broad Gauge
Std G 1881

B

A361

C

D

E

A361

F

G

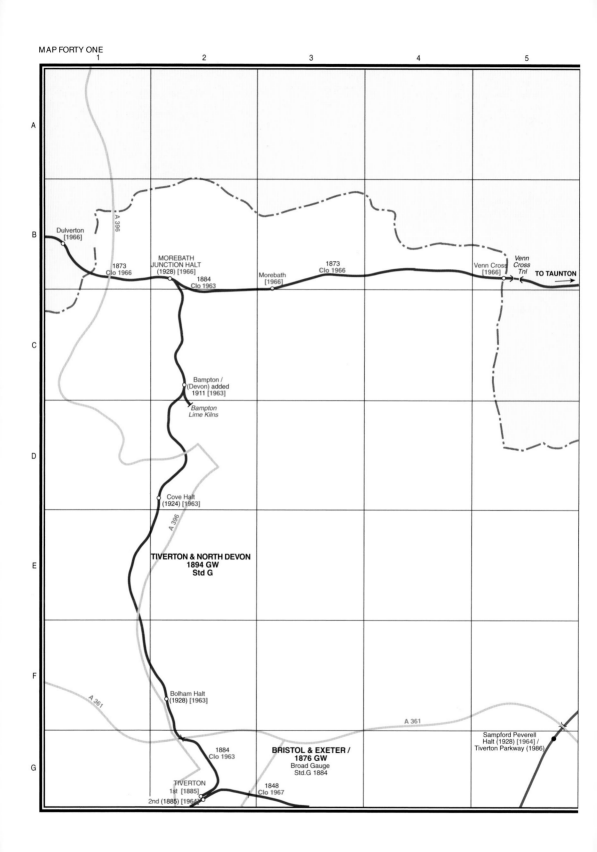

1   2   3   4   5

A

B

Dulverton
[1966]

A 396

1873
Clo 1966

MOREBATH
JUNCTION HALT
(1928) [1966]

1884
Clo 1963

Morebath
[1966]

1873
Clo 1966

Venn Cross
[1966]

Venn
Cross
Tnl

TO TAUNTON →

C

Bampton /
(Devon) added
1911 [1963]

*Bampton
Lime Kilns*

D

Cove Halt
(1924) [1963]

A 396

**TIVERTON & NORTH DEVON
1894 GW
Std G**

E

F

A 361

Bolham Halt
(1928) [1963]

A 361

Sampford Peverell
Halt (1928) [1964] /
Tiverton Parkway (1986)

G

1884
Clo 1963

**BRISTOL & EXETER /
1876 GW**
Broad Gauge
Std.G 1884

1848
Clo 1967

TIVERTON
1st [1885]
2nd (1885) [1964]

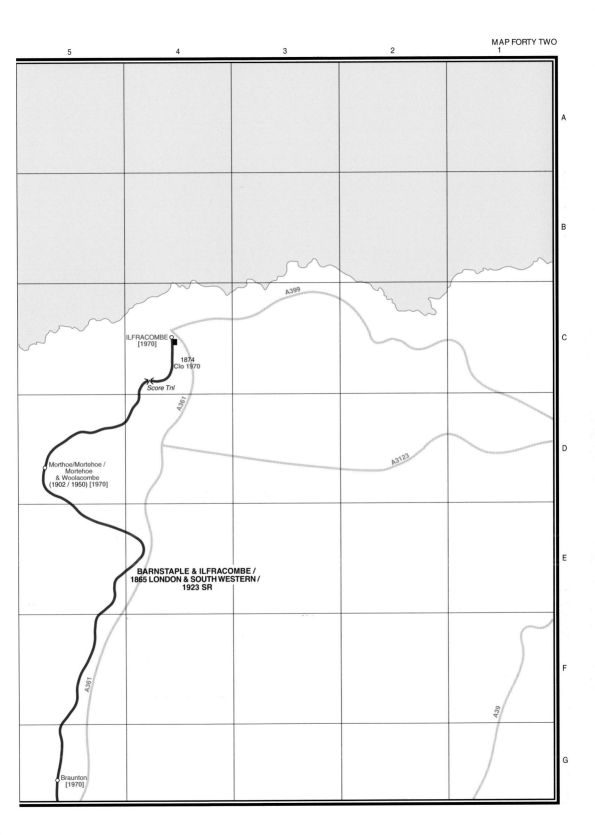

5   4   3   2   1

A

B

A399

ILFRACOMBE [1970]   C

1874
Clo 1970

Score Tnl

A361

Morthoe/Mortehoe /
Mortehoe
& Woolacombe
(1902 / 1950) [1970]

A3123   D

E

BARNSTAPLE & ILFRACOMBE /
1865 LONDON & SOUTH WESTERN /
1923 SR

A361

A39

F

G

Braunton
[1970]

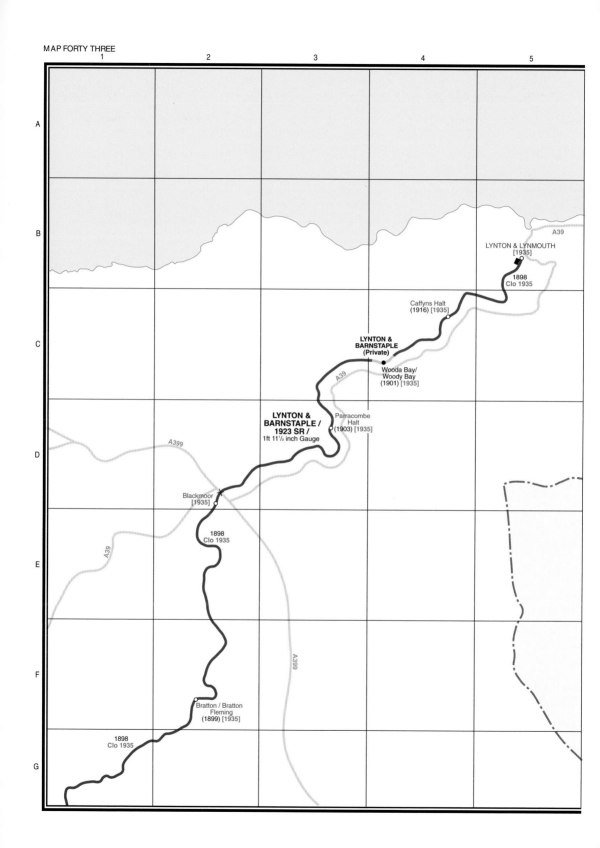

LYNTON & LYNMOUTH
[1935]

A39

1898
Clo 1935

Caffyns Halt
(1916) [1935]

**LYNTON &
BARNSTAPLE**
(Private)

A39

Wooda Bay/
Woody Bay
(1901) [1935]

**LYNTON &
BARNSTAPLE /
1923 SR /**
1ft 11½ inch Gauge

Parracombe
Halt
(1903) [1935]

A399

Blackmoor
[1935]

1898
Clo 1935

A39

A399

Bratton / Bratton
Fleming
(1899) [1935]

1898
Clo 1935

MAP INDEX AND GAZETTEER

Station	Map ref	Opened	Closed (passengers)	Closed (freight)
Abbotsham Road	37D1	20 May 1901	28 March 1917	n/a
Albert Quay	1G1	1869	n/a	1959
Albert Road Halt	10E5	1 November 1906	13 January 1947	n/a
Alphington Halt	27B4	2 April 1928	9 June 1958	n/a
Alphington Road Goods	27B4	1 July 1903	n/a	4 December 1967
Ambrosia Factory	17A3	1917	n/a	1970
Angarrack (first)	1D5	22 May 1843	16 February 1852	n/a
Angarrack (second)	1D5	16 February 1852	October 1853	n/a
Appledore	37C3	1 May 1908	28 March 1917	28 March 1917
Ashburton***	19D3	1 May 1872	3 November 1958	10 September 1962
Ashbury	24C3	20 January 1879	3 October 1966	7September 1964
Ashbury & North Lew	see Ashbury; known as Ashbury & North Lew April 1890 until Ashbury for North Lew 4 July 1937			
Ashbury for North Lew	see Ashbury; renamed post 1948			
Ashton****	27E1	9 October 1882	9 June 1958	1 May 1961
Ashwater	23D4	21 July 1886	3 October 1966	7 September 1964
Avonwick	12B5	19 December 1893	16 September 1963	11 June 1956
Axminster	30D2	19 July 1860	Open	18 April 1966*
Bampton (Devon)	41C2	1August 1884	7 October 1963	7 October 1963
Bampton	see Bampton (Devon); renamed June 1911			
Bampton Lime Kilns	41D2	1898	n/a	c1950
Barnstaple (Victoria Road)	38B4	1 November 1873	13 June 1960	5 March 1970
Barnstaple Junction	see Barnstaple; suffix carried 20 July 1874 until post 1970			
Barnstaple Quay	38B5	20 July 1874	16 May 1889	Unknown
Barnstaple Quay	see Barnstaple Town (first); renamed July 1886			
Barnstaple Town (first)	38B5	20 July 1874	16 May 1898	n/a
Barnstaple Town (second)	38B5	16 May 1898	5 October 1970	3 April 1940
Barnstaple	38B5	1 August 1854	Open	Unknown
Barnstaple	see Barnstaple (Victoria Road); renamed 26 September 1949			
Bayly's Wharf	10F3	1897	n/a	17 October 1961
Beach Road Halt	37C2	20 May 1901	28 March 1917	n/a
Beer Alston	see Bere Alston; renamed 18 November 1897			
Beer Ferris	see Bere Ferrers; renamed 18 November 1897			
Belstone Corner	see Sampford Courtenay; renamed 1 January 1872			
Bere Alston	9A5	2 June 1890	Open	28 February 1966
Bere Ferrers	10B5	2 June 1890	Open	8 October 1962
Bickleigh	10C2	22 June 1859	31 December 1962	31 December 1962
Bideford (first)	37D2	2 November 1855	10 June 1872	n/a
Bideford (Second)	37D2	10 June 1872	4 October 1965	6 September 1965
Bideford Quay	37D2	20 May 1901	28 March 1917	28 March 1917
Bideford (Yard) Halt	37D2	20 May 1901	28 March 1917	28 March 1917
Billacombe	10F2	17 January 1898	6 October 1947	29 February 1960
Bishop's Nympton & Molland	39D5	1 November 1873	3 October 1966	3 August 1964
Bissoe	3B2	30 January 1826	n/a	25 September 1915
Bittaford Platform	11E4	18 November 1907	2 March 1959	n/a
Blackmoor	43D2	11 May 1898	30 September 1935	30 September 1935
Bodmin General**	7A1/15G2	27 May 1887	31 January 1967	1 May 1967*
Bodmin North	7A1/15G1	1 November 1895	31 January 1967	29 November 1965
Bodmin Parkway	7B3	27 June 1859	Open	4 November 1963*
Bodmin Road	see Bodmin Parkway; renamed 4 November 1984			
Bodmin (GWR)	see Bodmin General; renamed 26 September 1949			
Bodmin (LSWR)	see Bodmin North; renamed 26 September 1949			
Bojea Sidings	6D2	1 May 1920	n/a	27 July 1964
Bolham Halt	41F2	23 April 1928	7 October 1963	n/a
Boscarne Exchange Platform	14G1	15 June 1964	30 January 1967	n/a
Boskell Sidings	6D2	24 May 1920	n/a	6 May 1968
Bovey	26G1	4 July 1866	2 March 1959	4 December 1967*
Bow	33B2	1 November 1865	5 June 1972	1 May 1961
Brampford Speke Halt	34F1	1 August 1884	7 October 1963	n/a
Brampford Speke	see Brampford Speke Halt; renamed 1 October 1923			
Bratton Fleming	43F2	11 May 1898	30 September 1935	30 September 1935
Bratton	see Bratton Fleming; renamed October 1899			
Braunton	42G5	20 July 1874	5 October 1970	7 September 1964
Brent	11C5	5 May 1848	5 October 1964	6 April 1964
Brentor	18B4	2 June 1890	6 May 1968	4 April 1960
Bridestowe	24F2	12 October 1874	6 May 1968	5 June 1961
Bridford Barytes Mine	27D1	1914	n/a	July 1958
Bridge Paper Mill	35E2	26 July 1894	n/a	31 August 1967
Bridges	see Luxulyan; renamed 1 May 1905			
Brimley Halt	19A5	21 May 1928	2 March 1959	n/a
Britannia Halt	13D3	c1897	Unk	n/a
Brixham Road	see Churston; renamed 1 May 1868			
Brixham	13B4	28 February 1868	13 May 1963	13 May 1963
Brixton Road	10F2	17 January 1898	6 October 1947+	29 February 1960
Broad Clyst	28A4	19 July 1860	7 March 1966	6 September 1965
Broad Clyst Permanent Way Depot	35G2	1896	n/a	1964
Brown Heath	11B4	1847	n/a	Unknown
Buckfastleigh**	19E2	1 May 1872	3 November 1958	10 September 1962
Bude Basin	22C3	10 August 1898	n/a	7 September 1964
Bude	22C2	10 August 1898	3 October 1966	7 September 1964
Budleigh Salterton	28E1	15 May 1897	6 March 1967	27 January 1964

Station	Map ref	Opened	Closed (passengers)	Closed (freight)
Budleigh	see East Budleigh; renamed 27 April 1898			
Bugle	6B2	20 June 1876	Open	1 June 1964*
Bullpoint Government Sidings	10D5	2 June 1916	n/a	c1990
Burlescombe	36B5	1867	5 October 1964	17 February 1964
Burn Halt	34C1	26 June 1926	7 October 1963	n/a
Burngullow (first)	6E3	1863	1 August 1901	n/a
Burngullow (second)	6E3	1 August 1901	14 September 1931	Uncertain (pre-1947)
Burrator Halt	18G2	4 February 1929	5 March 1956	n/a
Burrator Platform	see Burrator Halt; renamed 1929			
Cadbury Fry	27B4	31 December 1959	n/a	June 1970
Cadeleigh & Bickleigh	see Cadeleigh; renamed 1 May 1906			
Cadeleigh	34B1	1 May 1885	7 October 1963	7 October 1963
Caffyns Halt	43D4	December 1906	30 September 1935	n/a
Callington Road	see Callington; renamed 1 November 1909			
Callington	17G2	2 March 1908	7 November 1966	28 February 1966
Calstock Quay	9A5	8 May 1872	n/a	2 March 1908
Calstock	9A5	2 March 1908	Open	28 February 1966
Camborne	2C4	22 May 1843	Open	5 October 1964*
Camel's Head Halt	10E5	1 November 1906	4 May 1942	n/a
Camelford	21F3	14 August 1893	3 October 1966	7 September 1964
Cann Quarry	10D2	1854	n/a	1955
Cantilever (Military)	10E5	1905	May 1966	n/a
Carbean Siding	6C2	2 October 1893	n/a	29 April 1965
Carbis Bay	1D3	1 June 1877	Open	4 Jan 1965*
Carbis Wharf	6B3	1 June 1874	n/a	25 August 1989
Carharrack	3B1	30 January 1826	n/a	25 September 1915
Carloggas	6C4	1 July 1869	n/a	14 May 1992
Carn Brea	2B3	25 August 1852	2 January 1961	1 May 1967
Carn Quarry	10D2	30 January 1826	n/a	25 September 1915
Carne Point	7G3	1 June 1869	n/a	Open
Castle Hill	see Filleigh; renamed 1 January 1881			
Cattewater Harbour	10F4	1888	n/a	Open
Cattle Market	27B4	27 July 1939	n/a	c1965
Causeland Halt	see Causeland; suffix carried 21 September 1953 to 20 March 1967			
Causeland	8D3	11 September 1879	Open	n/a
Causeway Crossing Halt	37D2	20 May 1901	28 March 1917	n/a
Central Office (Military)	10E5	1900	May 1966	n/a
Chacewater	3A1	25 August 1852	5 October 1964	5 October 1964
Chapelton	38D4	1 August 1854	Open	4 Janaury 1965
Chapeltown	see Chapelton; closed 1860; reopened and renamed 1 March 1875			
Cheesewring Quarry	16F3	March 1846	n/a	1916
Chelfham	38A3	11 May 1898	30 September 1935	30 September 1935
Chilsworthy Halt	17F4	1 June 1909	7 November 1966	n/a
Cholwich Town	11B2	24 September 1858	n/a	c1910
Christow	27D1	1 July 1903	9 June 1958	1 May 1961
Chudleigh Knighton Halt	20A5	9 June 1924	9 June 1958	n/a
Chudleigh Road	see Heathfield; renamed I October 1882			
Chudleigh	27G2	9 October 1882	9 June 1958	4 December 1967
Churston**	13B3	14 March 1861	1 November 1972	4 December 1967
Clearbrook Halt	10A2	29 October 1958	31 December 1962	n/a
Clyst St Mary & Digby Halt	28B5	1 June 1908	27 September 1948	n/a
Colaton Raleigh Siding	29G1	Unknown	n/a	1 February 1953
Colcerrow Quarry	7E1	1841	n/a	1933
Coldharbour Halt	35A5/36D5	23 February 1929	9 September 1963	9 September 1963
Colesloggett Halt**	7B2	1992	Open	n/a
Collumpton	see Cullompston; renamed December 1867			
Colyford**	30F4	16 March 1868	7 March 1966	n/a
Colyton (first)	see Seaton Junction; renamed Colyton Junction 16 March 1868			
Colyton (second)**	30F4	16 March 1868	7 March 1966	3 February 1964
Colyton Junction	see Colyton; renamed 1 September 1869			
Colyton Town	see Colyton; renamed September 1890			
Combpyne	30F2	24 August 1903	29 November 1965	5 December 1960
Copperhouse Halt	1D4	1 July 1905	1 May 1908	n/a
Copperhouse	1D4	22 May 1843	16 February 1852	n/a
Cornborough Cliffs Halt	37D1	20 May 1901	28 March 1917	n/a
Cornwood	11D2	1852	2 March 1959	2 March 1959
Cornwood Road	see Cornwood; renamed April 1864			
Coryton	17B5	1 July 1865	31 December 1962	31 December 1962
Cove Halt	41D2	9 June 1924	7 October 1963	7 October 1963
Cownhawne**	30F4	Unknown	Open	n/a
Cox's Park Depot	see Latchley Halt; opened for goods traffic 8 May 1872; renamed 2 March 1908			
Crediton (first)	34F5	12 May 1851	1 August 1854	n/a
Crediton (second)	34F5	1 August 1854	Open	4 December 1967
Crockham Siding (Teign Valley Concrete works)	27F1	1904	n/a	4 December 1967
Cullompton	35B4	1 May 1844	5 October 1964	8 May 1967
Culm Valley Dairy	36C2	1920	n/a	October 1975
Culmstock	36C4	29 May 1876	9 September 1963	9 September 1963
Dainton Siding	20E5	by 1880	n/a	14 February 1965
Dartmouth**	13D2	16 August 1864	1 November 1972	n/a
Dawlish	20A2	30 May 1846	n/a	17 May 1965
Dawlish Warren (first)	28G5	1 July 1905	23 September 1912	n/a
Dawlish Warren (second)	28G5	23 September 1912	Open	5 August 1963
Defiance Halt	see Defiance Platform; renamed 1 May 1906			
Defiance Halt (workmen's)	9E4	1905	1908	n/a

Station	Map ref	Opened	Closed (passengers)	Closed (freight)
Defiance Platform	9E5	1 March 1905	27 October 1930	n/a
De Lank Quarry	15C2	1880	n/a	31 October 1966
Delabole	21G2	18 October 1893	3 October 1966	7 September 1964*
Delabole Slate Quarry	21G2	18 October 1895	n/a	January 1965
Devonport (Albert Road)	see Devonport; suffix carried 26 September 1949 to 6 May 1968			
Devonport (King's Road)	10E5	17 May 1876	7 September 1964	4 January 1971
Devonport (LSWR)	see Devonport (King's Road); renamed 26 September 1949			
Devonport	10E5	4 May 1859	Open	15 April 1957*
Devoran	3C3	30 January 1826	n/a	25 September 1915
Digby & Sowton	28B5	23 May 1994	Open	n/a
Dockyard Halt	see Dockyard; renamed 5 May 1969			
Dockyard	10E5	1 June 1905	Open	n/a
Dolcoath Halt	2C3	28 August 1905	1 May 1908	n/a
Doublebois	8B5	1860	5 October 1964	7 December 1964
Dousland	18G2	11 August 1883	5 March 1956	5 March 1956
Drakewalls Depot	see Gunnislae (1st); opened for goods traffic 8 May 1872 renamed 2 March 1908			
Drinnick Wharf	6C4	1 July 1869	n/a	Open
Dulverton	41B1	1 October 1873	3 October 1966	6 July 1964
Dunmere Halt	15F1	2 July 1906	30 January 1967	n/a
Dunsbear Halt	31C3	26 July 1925	1 March 1965	2 May 1960*
Dunsford Halt	27C1	16 January 1928	9 June 1958	n/a
Dunsland Cross	23A5	20 January 1879	3 October 1966	7 September 1964
East Anstey	40B3	1 November 1873	3 October 1966	30 September 1963
East Budleigh	28D1	15 May 1897	6 March 1967	27 January 1964
East Caradon Mine	16G2	1877	n/a	31 January 1916
East Wheal Rose Mine	5C2	26 February 1849	n/a	1905
East Yelland Power Station	37B3	1953	n/a	4 April 1973
Eggesford	32C3	1 August 1854	Open	4 January 1965
Egloskerry	22G2	4 October 1892	3 October 1966	9 May 1960
Elburton Cross	10F2	17 January 1897	6 October 1947+	n/a
Exeter City Basin	27B4	17 June 1867	n/a	6 September 1965*
Exeter Central	27A4	19 July 1860	Open	4 December 1967*
Exeter Electricity Works	27B4	2 March 1904	n/a	1 January 1963
Exeter Gas Works	27B4	5 November 1883	n/a	23 November 1973
Exeter Queen Street	see Exeter Central; renamed 1 July 1933			
Exeter St Davids	27A4	30 May 1846	Open	Unknown
Exeter St Thomas	27B4	30 May 1846	Open	n/a
Exminster	27D5	1852	30 March 1964	4 December 1967
Exmouth Docks	28F4	1868	n/a	31 December 1967
Exmouth (first)	28F4	1 May 1861	3 May 1976	4 December 1967
Exmouth (second)	28F4	3 May 1976	Open	n/a
Extension (Military)	10E5	1905	May 1966	n/a
Exton Halt	see Exton; suffix carried 28 February 1965 to 5 May 1969			
Exton	28D5	1 May 1861	Open	6 March 1961
Falmouth (first)	3F4 see Falmouth Docks; renamed 15 May 1989; station closed 7 December 1970 to 5 May 1975			
Falmouth (second)	see Falmouth Town; renamed The Dell 5 May 1975			
Falmouth Docks	3F4	24 August 1863	Open	4 January 1965*
Falmouth Docks	3F4	1861	n/a	Unknown
Falmouth Town	3F4	7 December 1970	Open	n/a
Feniton^^	29B1	19 July 1860	Open	6 March 1967
Filleigh	39C1	1 November 1873	3 October 1966	3 August 1964
Ford	see Ford (Devon); renamed 9 July 1923			
Ford (Devon)	10E5	2 June 1890	7 September 1964	1 September 1952
Ford Halt	10E5	1 June 1904	6 October 1941	n/a
Ford Platform	see Ford Halt; renamed 10 July 1922			
Fowey	7G3	16 September 1895	4 January 1965	1 June 1964*
Fremington	37B5	2 November 1855	6 September 1965	4 October 1965
Fremington Quay	37B5	2 November 1855	n/a	30 March 1970
Gara Bridge	12C4	19 December 1893	16 September 1963	16 September 1963
Gas House Siding	20G3	1866	n/a	6 December 1966
Geest Banana Store	20A5	April 1963	n/a	December 1975
Golant Halt	7F3	16 September 1895	4 January 1965	n/a
Golant	see Golant Halt; renamed 19 September 1955			
Goodrington Halt	see Goodrington Sands; renamed Goodrington Sands Halt 24 September 1928			
Goodrington Sands**	13A3	24 September 1928	1 November 1972	n/a
Goodrington Sands Halt	see Goodrington Sands; renamed 1 November 1972			
Goonbell Halt	4F3	14 August 1905	4 February 1963	n/a
Goonhavern Halt	4D1	14 August 1905	4 February 1963	n/a
Government Food Store	28A5	1942	n/a	1979
Grampound Road	5E5	4 May 1859	5 October 1964	1 June 1964
Gravel Hill Mine	4C1	1874	n/a	October 1888
Great Western Potteries & Brickworks (Candy's)		1887	n/a	1966
Grogley Halt	14F2	2 July 1906	30 January 1967	n/a
Gulf Oil Terminal	20A5	10 October 1966	n/a	17 January 1996
Gunheath Siding	6C3	2 October 1895	n/a	29 April 1965
Gunnislake (first)	17G4	2 March 1908	31 January 1994	28 February 1966
Gunnislake (second)	17G4	31 January 1994	Open	n/a
Gwinear	1D5	22 May 1843	16 February 1852	n/a
Gwinear Road	2C5	16 February 1852	5 October 1964	9 August 1965
Halberton Halt	35A3	5 December 1927	5 October 1964	n/a
Hale Mills	3B1	30 January 1826	n/a	25 September 1915
Halloon	see St Columb Road; renamed 1 November 1878			

Station	Map ref	Opened	Closed (passengers)	Closed (freight)
Halwill & Beaworthy	see Halwill; renamed Halwill Junction March 1887			
Halwill Junction	see Halwill; renamed 1 January 1923			
Halwill	24A5	20 January 1879	3 October 1966	7 September 1964
Hatherleigh	31F4	27 July 1925	1 March 1965	7 September 1964
Hawkmoor Halt	26F2 see Pullabrook Halt; renamed 13 June 1955			
Hayle (first)	1D4	22 May 1843	11 March 1852	n/a
Hayle (second)	1D4	11 March 1852	Open	8 June 1964*
Hayle Wharves	1D4	23 December 1837	n/a	1 May 1967*
Heathfield	20B	1874	2 March 1959	4 December 1967*
Hele & Bradninch	35D2	1 May 1844	5 October 1964	17 May 1965
Helston	2G3	9 May 1887	5 November 1962	5 October 1964
Hemerdon	11E1	Unknown	n/a	29 September 1902
Hemyock	36C2	29 May 1876	9 September 1963	6 September 1965*
Hendra Down	6C5	1852	n/a	Unknown
Higher Gothers Clayworks	6B4	1879	n/a	1931
Hole	31G2	27 July 1925	1 March 1965	7 September 1964
Holsworthy (first)	23A2	20 January 1879	11 August 1898	11 August 1898
Holsworthy (second)	23A2	11 August 1898	3 October 1966	7 September 1964
Horrabridge	18F3	22 June 1859	31 December 1962	31 December 1962
Ide	27B3	1 July 1903	9 June 1958	7 March 1955
Ilfracombe	42C4	20 July 1874	5 October 1970	7 September 1964
Ingra Tor Halt	18E2	2 March 1936	5 March 1956	n/a
Instow	37C3	2 November 1855	22 January 1968+++	4 October 1965
Ivybridge (first)	11E3	5 May 1848	2 March 1959	29 November 1965*
Ivybridge (second)	11E3	15 July 1994	Open	n/a
Kellybray	see Callington; opened for goods traffic 8 May 1872 renamed Callington Road 2 March 1908			
Kenwith Castle	37D1	20 August 1910	28 March 1917	n/a
Keyham	10E5	1 July 1900	Open	n/a
Keyham Admiralty Platform (Military)	10E5	1867	1954	n/a
Kilmar Quarry	16E3	1858	n/a	1898
King Tor Halt	18E1	2 April 1928	5 March 1956	n/a
King's Asphalt	27B4	24 June 1929	n/a	c1980
King's Nympton	31A4	1 August 1854	Open	4 December 1967
Kingsbridge Road	see Wrangaton; name carried May 1849 to 1 July 1895			
Kingsbridge	12G4	198 December 1893	16 September 1963	16 September 1963
Kingskerswell	20E4	1853	5 October 1964	5 August 1963
Kingswear**	13D3	16 October 1964	1 November 1972	4 May 1964*
Kithill Quarry	17F2	Unknown	n/a	December 1954
Laira Green	10E3	5 May 1848	2 April 1849	1 May 1849
Laira Halt	10E3	1 June 1904	7 July 1930	n/a
Lansalson	6C3	24 May 1920	n/a	27 July 1964
Lapford	32E2	1 August 1854	Open	4 December 1967
Latchley Halt	17F3	2 March 1908	7 November 1966	1949
Launceston (GW)	see Launceston North; renamed 18 June 1951			
Launceston (LSR)**	17A1	26 December 1983	Open	n/a
Launceston (LSW)	see Launceston South; renamed 18 June 1951			
Launceston North^^^	17A1	1 July 1865	30 June 1952	28 February 1966
Launceston South^^^	17A1	21 July 1886	3 October 1966	28 February 1966
Lee Moor	11B2	1854	n/a	1936
Lelant	1D3	1 June 1877	Open	May 1956
Lelant Halt	see Lelant; suffix carried 29 September 1959 to 5 May 1969			
Lelant Saltings	1E3	29 May 1978	Open	n/a
Lelant Wharf	1D4	1888	n/a	c1914
Liddaton Halt	19A5	4 April 1938	31 December 1962	n/a
Lifton	17A3	1 July 1865	31 December 1962	28 February 1966
Lion's Holt Halt	see St James Park; renamed St James Park Halt 7 October 1946			
Lipson Vale Halt	10E4	1 June 1904	22 March 1942	n/a
Liskeard (first)	8C3	4 May 1859	Open	30 April 1982
Liskeard (second)	8C3	15 May 1901	Open	n/a
Littleham	28F3	1 June 1903	6 march 1967	27 January 1964
Littlehempston Riverside**	see Totnes (Littlehempston)			
Loddiswell	see Loddiswell Halt; renamed 4 September 1961			
Loddiswell Halt	12E4	19 December 1893	16 September 1963	4 September 1961
Longdown	27B2	1 July 1903	9 June 1958	9 June 1958
Looe Quay	8G3	27 December 1860	n/a	23 March 1954
Looe	8F3	11 September 1879	Open	4 November 1963
Lostwithiel	7D2	4 May 1859	Open	1 June 1964*
Lover's Lane Halt	37C2	1 July 1908	28 March 1917	n/a
Lucas Terrace Halt	10E3	October 1905	10 September 1951	n/a
Luckett	17F3	2 March 1908	7 November 1966	10 September 1962
Lustleigh	26F2	4 July 1866	2 March 1959	6 April 1964
Luxulyan	6B1	20 June 1876	Open	1 June 1964*
Luxulyan Quarry	6B1	1855	n/a	c1880
Lidford (GW)	see Lydford (GW); renamed 3 June 1897			
Lidford (LSW)	see Lydford (LSWR); renamed 1 July 1897			
Lydford (GW)	18A4	1 July 1865	31 December 1962	31 December 1962
Lydford (LSW)	18A4	12 October 1874	6 May 1968	7 September 1964
Lyme Regis	30F1	24 August 1903	29 November 1965	3 February 1964
Lympstone Commando	28D4	3 May 1976	Open	n/a
Lympstone Halt	see Lympstone Village; suffix carried 28 February 1965 to 5 May 1969			
Lympstone Village	28E4	1 May 1861	Open	4 April 1960
Lympstone	see Lympstone Village; renamed 12 May 1991			
Lynton & Lynmouth	43B5	16 May 1898	30 September 1935	3 September 1935

Station	Map ref	Opened	Closed (passengers)	Closed (freight)
Maddaford Moor Halt	24C2	26 July 1926	3 October 1966	n/a
Marazion Road	see Marazion; renamed 24 June 1896			
Marazion	1G2	11 March 1852	5 October 1964	6 December 1965
Marke Valley Mine	16F3	August 1877	n/a	31 January 1916
Marland (North Devon Clay Co)	31C4	1880	n/a	12 September 1982
Marsh Barton	27B4	8 August 1958	n/a	Open
Marsh Mills	10E2	15 March 1961	31 December 1962	1 June 1964*
Marsh Mills China Clay Works	10D2	Unknown	n/a	Open
Mary Tavy & Blackdown	18C4	1 July 1865	31 December 1962	11 August 1941
Marytavy	see Mary Tavy & Blackdown; renamed Martytavy & Blackdown 1 May 1907			
Marytavy & Blackdown	see Mary Tavy & Blackdown; renamed unknown			
Meeth Halt	31E5	27 July 1925	1 March 1965	7 September 1964
Melangoose Mill	5C5	1 June 1874	n/a	April 1982
Meldon Quarry	25D1	c1895	n/a	Open
Meledor Mill	6D5	1 July 1912	n/a	April 1982
Menheniot	8D1	4 May 1859	Open	9 September 1963
Millbay Docks	10F4	Unknown	n/a	30 June 1971
Minions	16F3	1860	1886	Unknown
Minions Siding	16F3	Unknown	n/a	1 January 1917
Mithian Halt	4E3	14 August 1905	4 February 1963	n/a
Molland	see Bishop's Nympton & Molland; renamed 1March 1876			
Mollinis	6B2	1844	n/a	Unknown
Monks Corner Depot	see Luckett; opened for goods traffic 8 May 1872 renamed Stoke Climsland Road 2 March 1908			
Moorswater	8B4	11 September 1879	15 May 1901	16 December 1963*
Morchard Road	32F1/33A3	1 August 1854	Open	30 December 1963
Morchard Road Halt	see Morchard Road; suffix carried 12 September 1965 to 5 May 1969			
Morebath	41B3	1 November 1873	3 October 1966	3 June 1963
Morebath Junction Halt	41B2	1 December 1928	3 October 1966	n/a
Moretonhampstead	26D3	4 July 1866	2 March 1959	6 April 1964
Mortehoe & Woolacombe	42D4	20 July 1874	5 October 1970	7 September 1964
Mortehoe	see Mortehoe & Woolacombe; renamed 5 June 1950			
Morice Yard (Military)	10E5	1900	May 1966	n/a
Morthoe	see Mortehoe & Woolacombe; renamed Mortehoe 13 May 1902			
Morwellham Quay	9A5	1858	n/a	By December 1901
Mount Gould & Tothill Halt	10E3	2 October 1905	1 February 1918	n/a
Mount Hawke Halt	4G3	14 August 1905	4 February 1963	n/a
Mount Pleasant Road Halt	27A5	1906	2 January 1928	n/a
Mutley	10E4	1 August 1871	3 July 1939	n/a
Mutley (Plymouth)	see Mutley; renamed 28 March 1877			
Nancegollan	2F4	9 May 1887	5 November 1962	5 October 1964
Nangiles	3B2	Unknown	n/a	25 September 1915
Nanstallon Halt	14G1	2 July 1906	30 January 1967	n/a
New Caudledown South Siding	6B2	2 October 1893	n/a	September 1973
New Meledor Siding	6D5	11 October 1921	n/a	April 1982
New Mills**	17A2	June 1995	Open	n/a
Newham	3A4	16 April 1855	16 September 1963	8 November 1971
Newlyn	1G1	c1900	n/a	31 July 1972
Newquay Harbour	5A1	January 1849	n/a	1926
Newquay	5A1	20 June 1876	Open	7 September 1964
Newton Abbot	20C4	30 December 1846	Open	Unknown
Newton Poppleford	29F1	1 June 1899	6 March 1967	27 January 1964
Newton	see Newton Abbot; renamed 1 March 1877			
Newton St Cyres	34F3	12 May 1851	Open	12 September 1960
North Crofty Siding	2B3	23 December 1837	n/a	1 December 1948
North Kilmar Quarry	16E4	1879	n/a	1898
North Pool Siding	2B3	Unknown	n/a	Unknown
North Quay (GWR)	10F4	6 November 1879	n/a	3 December 1973
North Quay (LSWR)	10F4	22 October 1879	n/a	November 1950
North Roskear Siding	2B3	23 December 1837	n/a	1 December 1948
North Tawton**	25A5	1 November 1865	5 June 1972	7 September 1964
North Yard (Military)	10E5	1900	May 1966	n/a
Northam	37C2	20 May 1901	28 March 1917	n/a
Okehampton Road	see Sampford Courtenay; renamed Belstone Corner 3 October 1871			
Okehampton**	25C2	3 October 1971	5 June 1972	31 January 1983
Old Beam Siding (North Goonbarrow China Clay)	6B2	Unknown	n/a	20 March 1969
Oreston	10F3	5 September	10 September 1951	2 October 1961
Otterham	21E5	14 August 1893	3 October 1966	7 September 1964
Ottery Road	see Feniton; renamed Sidmouth Junction 6 July 1874			
Ottery St Mary	29D1	6 July 1875	6 March 1967	8 May 1967
Padstow Quay	14D5	27 March 1899	n/a	Pre 1953
Padstow	14D5	27 March 1899	30 January 1967	7 September 1964
Paignton	13A3	2 August 1859	Open	4 December 1967
Paignton Queens Park**	13A3	1974	Open	n/a
Par Harbour	7G1	1842	n/a	Open
Par	7F1	4 May 1859	Open	Unknown
Park Sidings (Admiralty then Esso)	35A4	1943	n/a	30 April 1983
Parkandillack	6C5	November 1849	n/a	Open
Parracombe Halt	43D3	November 1898	30 September 1935	n/a
Penlee Quarry	1G1	c1900	n/a	31 July 1972
Penmere Platform	see Penmere; renamed 5 May 1969			
Penmere	3F3	1 July 1925	Open	n/a
Penpol Siding	1D4	Unknown	n/a	Unknown
Penpoll	3C4	Unknown	n/a	25 September 1915

Station	Map ref	Opened	Closed (passengers)	Closed (freight)
Penponds	2C4	22 May 1843	16 February 1852	n/a
Penryn (first)	3E2	24 August 1863	24 June 1923	n/a
Penryn (second)	3E2	24 June 1923	Open	8 November 1971*
Pentewan Quay	6G2	June 1829	n/a	29 January 1918
Penzance	1G1	11 March 1852	Open	Unknown
Perran	see Perranwell; renamed 19 February 1864			
Perranporth Beach Halt	4D2	20 July 1931	4 February 1963	n/a
Perranporth	4D2	6 July 1903	4 February 1963	4 February 1963
Perranwell	3C3	24 August 1863	Open	4 January 1965
Petrockstow	31D4	27 July 1925	1 March 1965	7 September 1964
Phoenix Mine	16F3	1869	n/a	31 January 1916
Pilton Halt	38B5	16 May 1898	30 September 1935	n/a
Pilton Yard	see Pilton Halot; renamed 1904			
Pinhoe^	28A5	30 October 1871	Open	10 June 1967
Pitts Cleave Quarry	18D4	Unknown	n/a	1963
Plym Bridge Platform	10D2	1 May 1906	31 December 1962	n/a
Plymouth	10E4	28 March 1877	Open	Unknown
Plymouth	see Plymouth Millbay; renamed 1 May 1877			
Plymouth Friary	10F4	1 July 1891	15 September 1958	Unknown
Plymouth Millbay	10F4	2 April 1849	23 April 1941	20 June 1966*
Plymouth North Road	see Plymouth; renamed 15 September 1958			
Plympton	10E2	15 June 1848	2 March 1959	1 June 1964
Plymstock	10F3	5 September 1892	10 September 1951	7 October 1963
Plymstock Cement Works	10F3	c1963	n/a	Unknown
Pochins Siding	6B5	Unknown	n/a	Unknown
Point Quay	3C4	1827	n/a	25 September 1915
Poldice	3B1	c1812	unk	c1865
Poldice Mine	3B1	1854	n/a	25 September 1915
Polsloe Bridge Halt	see Polsloe Bridge; renamed 5 May 1969			
Polsloe Bridge	27A5	1907	Open	n/a
Poltimore Brick Siding	28A5	Unknown	n/a	6 September 1965
Polwrath	16G3	Unknown	n/a	Unknown
Ponts Mill	7F1	Unknown	n/a	Open
Pool	see Carn Brea; renamed unknown			
Port Isaac Road	14B1	1 June 1895	3 October 1966	7 September 1964
Portreath	2A3	23 December 1837	n/a	1 April 1938
Portreath (Poldice Tramway)	2A3	c1812	unknown	c1865
Portsmouth Arms	38G2	1 August 1854	Open	3 July 1961
Praze	2E4	9 May 1887	5 November 1962	5 October 1964
Preston Platform	20G3	24 July 1911	21 September 1914	n/a
Princetown	18E1	11 August 1883	5 March 1956	5 March 1956
Probus & Ladock Platform	5F4	1 February 1908	2 December 1957	n/a
Pullabrook Halt	26F2	1 June 1931	2 March 1959	n/a
Pye Storage Ltd Sidings	28A5	n/a	n/a	March 1968
Quintrel Downs Platform	see Quintrel Downs; renamed unknown			
Quintrel Downs	5A2	1911	Open	n/a
Redlake	11B2	11 September 1911	n/a	1932
Redruth (first)	2B2	22 May 1843	25 August 1852	1 May 1967
Redruth (R&C)	2B1	30 January 1826	n/a	25 September 1915
Redruth (second)	2B2	25 August 1852	Open	17 June 1912
Respryn	7C2	4 May 1859	Post August 1864	n/a
Retew	5C5	1882	n/a	1972
Richmond Road Halt	37C2	1 May 1908	28 March 1917	n/a
Roche	6A3	20 June 1876	Open	1 June 1964
Rolle Quay	38A5	23 February 1861	n/a	7 September 1964
Ruthern Bridge	14G2	6 August 1834	30 December 1933++	1 January 1934
St Agnes	4F4	6 July 1903	4 February 1963	4 February 1963
St Austell	6D2	4 May 1859	Open	4 March 1918
St Blazey	7F1	20 June 1876	21 September 1925	1 June 1964
St Budeaux Ferry Road	10D5	1 May 1906	Open	n/a
St Budeaux Platform	see St Budeaux Ferry Road 26 September 1949			
St Budeaux Victoria Road	10D5	2 June 1890	Open	11 December 1961*
St Budeaux Victoria Road Halt	see St Budeaux Victoria Road; suffix carried 18 July 1965 to 5 May 1969			
St Budeaux	see St Budeaux Victoria Road; renamed 26 September 1949			
St Columb Brick Works	5B5	Unknown	n/a	Unknown
St Columb Road	5B5	20 June 1876	Open	7 September 1964
St Cyres	see Newton St Cyres; renamed 1 October 1913			
St Erth	1E3	11 March 1852	Open	1 May 1967
St Germans	9E2	4 May 1859	Open	19 July 1965
St Germans Viaduct (workmen's0	9E3	1905	1908	n/a
St Ives Road	see St Erth; renamed 1 June 1877			
St Ives (first)	1C2	1 June 1877	23 May 1971	9 September 1963
St Ives (second)	1C2	23 May 1971	Open	n/a
St James Park Halt	see St James Park; renamed 5 May 1969			
St James Park	27A4	1906	Open	n/a
St Kew Highway	14D1	1 June 1895	3 October 1966	7 September 1964
St Keyne	8D3	1902	Open	n/a
St Keyne Halt	see St Keyne; suffix carried 21 September 1953 to 20 March 1967			
St Lawrence Platform	15G1	26 October 1906	1 January 1917	n/a
St Neot's China Clay Works	8B4	1904	n/a	1996
St Thomas	see Exeter St Thomas; renamed May 1897			
St Thomas, Exeter	see Exeter St Thomas; renamed St Thomas April 1853			
Saltash	9E5	4 May 1859	Open	9 September 1963
Salterton	see Budleigh Salterton; renamed 27 April 1898			

Station	Map ref	Opened	Closed (passengers)	Closed (freight)
Sampford Courtenay**	25B3	8 January 1867	5 June 1972	3 April 1961
Sampford Courtenay Halt	see Sampford Courtenay; suffix carried 12 September 1965 to 5 May 1969			
Sampford Peverell Halt	41G5	9 July 1928	5 October 1964	n/a
Sandplace	8E3	December 1881	Open	18 June 1951
Sandplace Halt	see Sandplace; suffix carried 21 September 1953 to 20 March 1967			
Saw Milling & General Supplies	387B5	World War 1	n/a	30 November 1967
Scorrier Gate	see Scorrier; suffix carried 25 August 1852 to 1856 and from 1859 to 1 October 1896			
Scorrier	2A1	25 August 1852	5 October 1964	n/a
Scraesdon Fort	9F3	c1893	n/a	c1903
Seaton	30G4	16 March 1868	7 March 1966	3 February 1964
Seaton Junction	30E4	19 July 1860	7 March 1966	8 May 1967*
Seven Stones Halt	17F3	15 June 1910	September 1917	n/a
Shaugh Bridge Platform	10B2	19 October 1907	21 December 1962	n/a
Shipley Bridge	11C5	1847	n/a	Unknown
Shooting Range Platform	14F2	c1885	1947	n/a
Sidmouth Junction	see Feniton; station closed 6 March 1967; renamed and reopened 5 May 1971			
Sidmouth	29F2	6 July 1874	6 March 1967	8 May 1967
Silverton	35E2	1867	5 October 1964	3 May 1965*
Snapper Halt	38A3	1903	30 September 1935	n/a
South Caradon	16G3	28 November 1844	n/a	31 January 1916
South Hams Brick Works	10G2	Unknown	n/a	Unknown
South Molton Road	see King's Nympton; renamed 1 March 1951			
South Molton	39D3	1 November 1873	3 October 1966	3 August 1964
South Western Gas Board (Truro)	3A4	3 April 1955	n/a	25 December 1970
South Yard (Military)	10E5	1900	May 1966	n/a
Starcross	28F5	30 May 1846	Open	4 December 1967
Staverton	see Staverton Bridge; reopened and renamed by Dart Valley Railway 5 April 1969			
Staverton Bridge**	19F4	1 May 1872	3 November 1958	10 September 1962
Steer Point	10G1	17 January 1898	6 October 1947+	29 September 1960
Stenalees	6C2	2 October 1893	n/a	1965
Stoke Canon (first)	34F1	1860	2 July 1894	n/a
Stoke Canon (second)	34F1	2 July 1894	13 June 1960	3 May 1965
Stoke Climsland	see Luckett; renamed 1 November 1909			
Stonehouse Pool	10F5	1877	n/a	1966
Stoneycombe Sidings	20E4	1883	n/a	5 May 1982
Strand Road Halt	37D2	20 August 1901	28 March 1917	n/a
Sutton Harbour	10F4	1852	n/a	31 December 1973
Swimbridge	38C2	1 November 1873	3 October 1966	3 August 1964
Tamerton Foliot	10C5	22 December 1897	10 September 1962	October 1956
Tamerton Foliott	see Tamerton Foliot; renamed June 1906			
Tavistock (GW)	see Tavistock South; renamed 26 September 1949			
Tavistock (LSW)	see Tavistock North; renamed 26 September 1949			
Tavistock North	18D5	2 June 1890	6 May 1968	28 February 1966
Tavistock South	18E5	22 June 1859	31 December 1962	7 September 1964
Teign House Siding	27D1	1882	n/a	12 July 1903
Teignbridge Siding	20B4	14 June 1892	n/a	14 June 1965*
Teigngrace Halt	20B5	December 1876	2 March 1959	28 May 1962
Teigngrace	see Teigngrace Halt; renamed 8 May 1939			
Teignmouth	20B1	30 May 1846	Open	4 December 1967
Texaco Siding (Exeter)	27B4	7 November 1966	n/a	21 July 1983
The Dell	see Falmouth Town; renamed 15 May 1989			
The Lane Halt (also known as				
Chanters Lane Halt)	37D2	20 August 1901	28 March 1917	n/a
Thorverton	34E1	1 May 1885	7 October 1963	4 May 1964*
Thorverton Mill (E.J. Coombe Ltd)	34E1	1899	n/a	30 November 1966
Ticket Platform (Bodmin)	7B1	1897?	By July 1902	n/a
Ticket Platform (Churston)	13B3	1897?	By July 1902	n/a
Ticket Platform (Exeter)	27A4	June 1873	Unk	n/a
Ticket Platform (Exmouth)	28F4	June 1873	Unk	n/a
Ticket Platform (Gwinear Road)	2C5	16 February 1862	1 January 1903	n/a
Ticket Platform (Helston)	2G3	9 May 1887	1 January 1903	n/a
Ticket Platform (Kingswear)	13D3	July 1897	By November 1915	n/a
Ticket Platform (Moretonhampstead)	13B3	4 July 1886	By July 1902	n/a
Ticket Platform (Penzance)	1G1	July 1897	By January 1905	n/a
Ticket Platform (St Erth)	1E3	July 1897	1 January 1903	n/a
Ticket Platform (St Ives)	1C2	July 1897	1 January 1903	n/a
Tipton St Johns	29E1	6 July 1874	6 March 1967	27 January 1964
Tipton	see Tipton St Johns; renamed 2 January 1881			
Tiverton (first)	41G2	12 June 1848	1 May 1885	n/a
Tiverton (second)	41G2	1 May 1885	5 October	5 June 1967
Tiverton Junction	35A4	1 May 1844	12 May 1986	8 May 1967*
Tiverton Parkway	41G5	12 May 1986	Open	n/a
Tiverton Road	see Tiverton Junction; renamed 12 June 1848			
Tokenbury Corner Depot	16G3	1861	n/a	31 January 1916
Topsham Quay	28C5	23 September 1861	n/a	1957
Topsham	28C5	1 May 1861	Open	4 December 1967
Torquay (first)	see Torre; renamed 2 August 1859			
Torquay (second)	20F3	2 August 1859	Open	n/a
Torre	20F3	18 December 1848	Open	4 December 1967
Torrington	37G3	18 July 1872	4 October 1865	6 September 1965*
Totnes (Littlehempston)**	19G4	5 April 1969	Open	n/a
Totnes Quay	12A1	1873	n/a	December 1969
Totnes Riverside	see Totnes (Littlehempston); renamed Littlehempston Riverside 1988			
Totnes	12A2	20 July 1847	Open	4 December 1967*
Totness	see Totnes; renamed December 1866			
Tower Hill	23F3	21 July 1886	3 October 1966	6 January 1964

Station	Map ref	Opened	Closed (passengers)	Closed (freight)
Treamble	4C1	1874	n/a	2 January 1905*
Tregantle Fort	9G3	c1893	n/a	c1903
Tremabe	8A3	Unknown	n/a	Unknown
Tresavean Mine	2C1	1838	n/a	1 January 1936
Tresmeer	22F4	28 July 1892	3 October 1966	7 September 1964
Tresarrett Siding	15D2	1834	n/a	July 1970
Trevemper Siding	5B1	Unknown	n/a	28 October 1963
Truro Road	3A4	25 August 1852	16 April 1855	n/a
Truro	3A4	4 May 1852	Open	Unknown
Trusham	27F1	9 October 1882	9 June 1958	5 April 1965
Truthall Halt	see Truthall Platform; renamed 1 July 1906			
Truthall Platform	2G3	3 July 1905	5 November 1962	n/a
Turnchapel	10F3	5 September 1892	10 September 1951	2 October 1961
Turnchapel Wharves	10F4	1897	n/a	30 October 1961
Twelve Heads	3B2	30 January 1826	n/a	25 September 1915
Uffculme	36D5	29 May 1876	9 September 1963	8 May 1967*
Umberleigh	38E3	1 August 1854	Open	4 January 1965
Up Exe	see Up Exe Halt; renamed 1 October 1923			
Up Exe & Silverton	see Up Exe Halt; renamed Up Exe 1 May 1905			
Up Exe Halt	34D1	1 May 1885	7 October 1963	n/a
Venn Cross	41B5	1 November 1873	3 October 1966	30 September 1963
Victoria	see Roche; renamed 1 May 1904			
Wacker Quay	9F3	c1893	n/a	c1903
Wadebridge (first)	14E3	4 July 1834	3 September 1888	3 September 1888
Wadebridge (second)	14E3	3 September 1888	30 January 1967	4 September 1978
Wadebridge Quay	14E3	4 July 1834	n/a	2 April 1973
Warren Halt	see Dawlish Warren (first); renamed 1 October 1911			
Warren's Siding	28F4	Late 19th century	n/a	1950s
Watergate Halt	31A2	27 July 1925	1 March 1965	2 May 1960
Wearde Siding (workmen's)	9E4	1905	1908	n/a
Wenford Bridge	15C2	30 September 1834	1 November 1886	18 November 1983
West Caradon Mine	16G3	Unknown	n/a	31 January 1916
West Exe Halt	35A1	19 March 1928	7 October 1963	n/a
Westleigh	36B5	1873	n/a	c1961
Weston Milton Halt	see Weston Milton; renamed 5 May 1969			
Weston Milton	10D5	3 July 1933	Open	n/a
Westward Ho!	37C1	20 May 1901	28 March 1917	28 March 1917
Wheal Anna Maria	17F4	c1856	n/a	By December 1901
Wheal Beacham	2C2	c1826	n/a	25 September 1915
Wheal Buller Mine	2C2	c1826	n/a	25 September 1915
Wheal Emma	17F5	c1856	n/a	By December 1901
Whetcombe Quarry Siding	27D1	1910	n/a	1931
Whimple	35F4	19 July 1860	Open	4 December 1967*
Whitchurch Down Platform	18E4	1 September 1906	31 December 1962	n/a
Whitehall Halt	36C3	27 February 1933	9 September 1963	n/a
Whitstone & Bridgerule	22A2	1 November 1898	3 October 1966	7 September 1964
Wingfield Villas Halt	10E5	1 June 1904	June 1921	n/a
Wivelscombe (workmen's)	9E3	1905	1908	n/a
Wooda Bay	see Woody Bay; renamed 1901			
Woodbury Road	see Exton; renamed 15 September 1958			
Woody Bay**	43C4	16 May 1898	30 September 1935	30 September 1935
Wrafton	37A4	20 July 1874	5 October 1970	7 September 1964
Wrangation	11D5	5 May 1848	2 March 1959	9 September 1963
Yarde Halt	31B3	1 August 1926	1 March 1965	n/a
Yealmpton	11G1	17 January 1898	6 October 1947+	29 February 1960
Yelverton	10A2	1 May 1885	31 December 1962	n/a
Yeo Mill Halt	40B4	27 June 1932	3 October 1966	n/a
Yeoford	33C4	1 August 1854	Open	10 February 1964
Yeoford Junction	see Yeoford; renamed post 1948			

* Closed for all goods traffic except private sidings; these closed later.
** Station now preserved.
*** Station reopened 5 April 1969 by the Dart Valley Railway but closed again on 2 October 1971 as a result of roadwork between Buckfastleigh and Ashburton.
**** Following flooding of the line on 30 September 1960 the station no longer received traffic by rail.
+ Station closed between 7 July 1930 and 3 November 1941.
++ Station closed between 1 November 1886 and 1 November 1895.
+++ Station closed 4 October 1965 to 10 January 1968.
^ Station closed 7 March 1966 to 16 May 1983.
^^ Station closed from 6 March 1967 (as Sidmouth Junction) to 3 May 1971.
^^^ The suffixes 'North' and 'South' only used in connection with the two goods depots in the town.